D0005941

BLACK DIAMONDS
AND
THE BLUE BRAZIL

In Memory
Alex Westwater, Robert Holman,
George S. Hutchison
Joe and Ina Ferguson

In Hope
Fiona, Neil, Alasdair Ferguson
that their Season may be
a memorable one

For everything there is a season,
and a time for every matter under heaven:
a time to be born, and a time to die;
a time to plant, and a time to pluck up what is planted;
a time to kill, and a time to heal;
a time to break down, and a time to build up;
a time to weep, and a time to laugh;
a time to mourn, and a time to dance...
What gain has the worker from his toil?
(Ecclesiastes 3. 1-9)

Here for a season, then above

— *Revised Church Hymnary, No 79*

© Copyright 1993, Ronald Ferguson. Not to be reproduced in any form without written authorisation from the publishers. Photographs reproduced by kind permission of:– pp. 38, 65, 81, 192 – DC Thomson; pp. 67, 85, 138 – The Dunfermline Press; p. 175 – News International.

Printed and published by Famedram Publishers, Ellon, Aberdeenshire

Here for a Season . . . .

Black Diamonds and the Blue Brazil

A Chronicle of Coal, Cowdenbeath and Football

RONALD FERGUSON

Northern Books
from Famedram

The Author

RONALD FERGUSON was brought up in Cowdenbeath, and worked for seven years in journalism in Fife and Edinburgh. He graduated MA with Honours in History and Philosophy from St Andrews University, and gained a First Class Honours Theology degree at Edinburgh University. After post graduate work in the States, gaining the degree of Master of Theology, he worked for eight years as a Church of Scotland minister in Easterhouse, Glasgow. After seven years as Leader of the Iona Community, he became minister of St Magnus Cathedral, Orkney.

He is the author of several books, including *Geoff* (published by Famedram), *Grace and Dysentery* and *Chasing the Wild Goose*. His best-selling biography, *George MacLeod,* commissioned by Collins and published in 1990, saw him shortlisted for the McVities £5000 Scottish Writer of the Year award.

His short fiction and poetry have been published in the Glasgow *Herald,* and his one-man play, *Every Blessed Thing,* was premièred by Tom Fleming at the St Magnus Festival in 1993. He is married to Cristine and has three of a family, Fiona, Neil and Alasdair.

Contents

Preface

I HAVE wanted to write a book about Cowdenbeath and football for some years. We all have our ambitions.

When I put up the notion to Collins, who had published two of my respectable books, they were fazed by the very idea. There is a flaw here, they said, relentlessly. If Cowdenbeath is the worst supported team in Britain, who will buy the book? Such logic is, of course, irritating. Other publishers responded in the kindly, solicitous tones used by earnest counsellors when dealing with demented clients. But then came the handsome, discerning and talented *(will this do?)* Bill Williams of Famedram, a man who knows a loony when he meets one. This is so bizarre that I must publish it, was the gist of his excited verdict. This book could become cult.

Black Diamonds and the Blue Brazil takes a season in Cowdenbeath Football Club's gloriously tortured history – it could have been any season, but it in the event it turned out to be an extraordinary season by any standards, one which grabbed the attention of the British media – and with that shaky, circular loom a pattern of a kind is woven. The football season is a useful vehicle, since human history is linear and cyclical at the same time: we understand this in our hearts even if we can't yet get it sorted out in our heads.

This particular West Fife wheel, stained as it is with blood and dusted with black grime, represents defiant history from the point of view of some of its losers, rather than from the much-hyped vantage point of the high, polished wheel of the orthodox juggernaut. It is, in the words of Stuart Cosgrove – describing his wonderfully entertaining *Hampden Babylon* – an unashamedly provincial book, written from the heart and soul of the other Scotland, that bit of forgotten countryside where the pies outnumber the fans. It is sado-masochistic history.

I wrote this story in conjunction with my son Neil, who was my research man. With a book like this, one is dependent on the memories and labours and hospitality of many others, and my thanks are due to in particular to Helen Peace, Frank Dillon, Alan Hutchison and Mark Ianson, and the various contributors to the histories of Cowdenbeath. A special mention must be made of the contribution provided by David Allan, author of *Fifeshire Football Memories* and *There was a Happy Land*. His knowledge is exceptional: in checking out my own memories and researches I simply had to refer to David, though no errors in the text should be attributed to him or to any of the others mentioned.

A special word of gratitude, too, to Jim Stark, editor of the *Central Fife Times*, and to Douglas Spence, the librarian at the *Courier* for their indefatigable researches. Thanks are also due to the *Central Fife Times*, the *Courier*, the *Scotsman*, the *Herald* and the *Sun* for permission to reproduce photographic and other material, and to publishers Stanley Paul for permission to use quotes from *The Party's Over* by Jim Baxter.

A special thank-you, too, to my long-suffering congregation in St Magnus Cathedral, Kirkwall ("Why is the minister always talking about Cows and Beef?" inquired one bewildered young Sunday School lad of his confused parents). Quite soon after I went to St Magnus, I predicted at the beginning of the season that Cowdenbeath would win promotion to the First Division for the first time in more than twenty years. A profound and moving silence descended upon all who heard. This was a prophecy of such stunning yet apocalyptic obscurity that many people, who had never even heard of such a place or team, were startled. Could it have been recorded in the Book of Revelation? Elderly ladies who had taken no interest in football found themselves transfixed each week by the Second Division results, becoming most upset when Cowdenbeath lost. And when the season went right to the wire, to the very last game, the excitement was unbearable. The rest, as they say, is history: suffice it to observe that my reputation as the Nostradamus of the North was spectacularly established.

In the meantime, I look forward to seeing how this work will be classified by the booksellers. Sport? Politics? Religion? Autobiography? Jewellery? South American Travel? My little book about Iona, *Chasing the Wild Goose,* has been spotted in bookshops under the various headings of Religion, Wild Life, Children's Stories and Scottish History, and once sat primly but proudly between *The Hip and Thigh Diet* and *The Joy of Sex.*

See us Renaissance Men from West Fife?

RON FERGUSON

Signing session for Ron Ferguson's best selling *George MacLeod*

Foreword

Without Prejudice*
*as the lawyers say

FOR YEARS I have felt an enhanced status in the presence of
Ron Ferguson. There are not many people in this world a Partick
Thistle fan can safely patronise; thus a friend who is a
Cowdenbeath supporter is a rare treasure.

As a lifelong Thistle fan, I learned early on about lowly status.
At a 'Proddy' primary school where, even within shouting distance of Firhill, the bulk of the boys supported Rangers, we Jags
supporters were a tolerated and patronised minority.

But, I well remember, we knew about 'real' truth, and in the
face of any amount of derision we could nurse that 'truth' in our
souls, ennobling the face we presented to the world. Their big
hero was 'Deedle-dawdle', Willie Waddell, but we knew Johnny
McKenzie was far superior. That one truth more than made up for
all their league championships and Scottish cups and the rest.
Johnny McKenzie was truly the greatest, the quintessential
Maryhill Magyar! We knew that and they didn'y!

One night, a few years ago, in his house in Govan in the
shadow of the new Ibrox Stadium, when we sat discussing the
future of the world or something like that as clergymen are prone
to do, Ron got on to talking about his dream of writing a book
about Cowdenbeath FC, the Blue Brazil. Well, even if this
sounded barmy beyond belief, I was drinking his whisky at the
time, so it seemed a reasonable thing to hear him out.

Up, out of his chair he got, and started to tell me about his
father's stories of 'Hooky' Leonard. As Ron held on to the
mantlepiece to demonstrate the arthritic nature of his father's
description of the flowing way in which the legendary Hooky
could bring down a ball with his thigh and move forward with

9

great grace, I began to hear echoes of my own long-held 'truth' about Johnny McKenzie.

The comparisons between past and present and the recalling of the names of the 'greats' of Cowdenbeath, intermingling with the revered heroes of Firhill, filled the room with a litany of praise and thanksgiving which transported this pair of middle-aged romantics to the mountaintop of hope fortified by selective memory and good whisky.

Is it not a triumph of the human spirit that we can leap in a single memory from a mix of the classical Hungarians and magical Brazilians to Partick Thistle and Cowdenbeath? Is it not a thing of wonder that talk of Puskas and Hideguti and of Jarzhino and Pele can lead naturally to Johnny McKenzie and Jimmy McGowan and to Hooky Leonard and Aly Venters?

It is a seamless garment, mysterious and mystical, this fellowship of the terracing that has created gods of and for the sons of Glasgow tenements, Fife mining villages, Brazilian beaches and European capitals over which armies have marched many times in a single lifetime. It is a canvas, a manuscript, a prayer. It is our expression of art and passion, the individual dream and despair, the collective ecstasy and agony.

It is here in these pages. Read and enjoy them, and dream a little....dream a lot.

ERIK CRAMB
Industrial chaplain, Dundee, and official chaplain to the Tartan Army at the European finals in Sweden, 1992.

Introduction

*My grandfather was paralysed. Once he was asked to tell
a story about his teacher, and he told how the holy Baal
Shem Tov used to jump and dance when he was praying.
My grandfather stood up when he was telling the story,
and the story carried him away so much that he had to
jump and dance to show how the master had done it. From
that moment he was healed.* – Jewish Hassidic tale

Insanity is hereditary: you can get it from your children.
– Sam Levenson

MY FATHER, when he was into his eighties, would risk severe
injury to himself by demonstrating how 'Hooky' Leonard used to
bring down the ball and pass it in one sweeping movement. Stiff,
puffed out, and suffering from angina, Joe Ferguson would stand
precariously on one leg, balancing himself against the table,
stretch out the other creaking limb till near waist height, and pull
down an imaginary ball – which was gracefully passed out to the
right wing (somewhere between the armchair and the television
set).

It mattered to him. James Leonard, one of Cowdenbeath's
legendary heroes, was simply peerless. A genius. A folk hero.
When will we see his likes again?

It was back in 1923 – the beginning of the club's Golden Era –
that Cowdenbeath plunged into the transfer market and paid a
whole fiver to Saltcoats Victoria for Hooky. He was paid £1 10/- a
week. A great crowd pleaser who seemed to have the ball tied to
his instep, Hooky scored eighty four goals for Cowden. His
indiscipline on and off the field was as bad as his ball skills were
brilliant (was he reincarnated as local hero Jim Baxter?) He was
suspended in 1925 for missing training sessions. The club insisted

that he live in Cowdenbeath, where they could keep an eye on him. He was demoted to the reserves "for failing to keep himself fit on Friday nights." One can only imagine what that state of Friday evening unfitness was like. In 1926 he walked out on Cowden to cross the Atlantic and play for Indiana Flooring in the US football league. When he returned to Cowdenbeath the following season, he received a ten week suspension and a £25 fine from the Scottish Football Association for breaking his contract. His form with Cowdenbeath was again brilliant and several big clubs, including Arsenal, wanted to sign him. But Hooky decided to return to the States to play in New York.

Once again, the lure of the fleshpots of Cowdenbeath proved too much for Hooky, and in 1929 he found himself back among the West Fife pit bings for the third time. The following year, when Cowdenbeath beat Morton 2-1 at Greenock, Hooky's tormenting of the home defence led him to being stoned by the local fans (the Greenock ground was closed for a fortnight, and Morton were fined £25 by the SFA). Leonard had the consolation of soon being selected for the Scottish League against the Irish League, along with the Cowdenbeath goalkeeper Bob Middleton. Immediately afterwards, Hooky was transferred to Sunderland for a fee of £3000 – a very substantial return on the original £5 investment.

There are others like Hooky, and they swagger and strut or limp through the pages of this book: characters such as Willie Devlin, Willie Pullar, Willie Rankin and Willie Stewart (in a memorable Cowdenbeath side that had eight Williams in their ranks), and Cowden's Egyptian inside forward Tewfick Abdullah (nicknamed 'Toothpick') who had a local greyhound named after him. Their name is legion and their name is legend.

All this was more than sixty years ago, in the days when West Fife miners went straight from the pithead to the playing field. When a player went down injured, his rubbed back would be black with coal dust. The football was passionate and skilful, played in front of big, partisan crowds. Men still worked Saturday mornings, in the days before buses carried the Flower of Scotland from towns and villages to support the successful and glamorous Old Firm of Rangers and Celtic. It was also the days when miners had work. Cowdenbeath, nicknamed 'the Chicago of Fife' at the turn of the century, was a small-scale boom town based not on gold, but on 'black diamonds'. It mushroomed during the coal rush, and its football club owes its origin to the precious 'black stanes that burned'.

The signs and scars of mining were everywhere – the colliery wheels and pit bings – and the subsidence caused by mine workings meant that bits of the town were slowly sinking. (One day a horse pulling a milk cart simply disappeared down a hole which suddenly opened up in the road before it. It was possible to walk in parts of Cowdenbeath and feel that you were drowning, even if you were on dry land.)

It was a gritty, compassionate community which closed ranks when adversity struck – and it struck often. The true price of the black diamonds could only be measured in red human blood. Cowdenbeath was a community which knew how to wait – in silence at the pithead gates as the high, idle wheels testified mutely to death down below. It was also a community which knew how to struggle. Young people were reared on the stories of union battles with the Fife Coal Company: of strikes, lockouts, banning, imprisonment.

Most of the people in the town made their living from the pits, either directly or indirectly. My father was no exception. Having left school at 13, he worked in the family painter and decorator's business, making extra money by inscribing names on coffins in elegant copperplate painted letters. The fortunes of the decorating trade rose or fell with the economics of King Coal, as did the fortunes of the football club.

The stability of that community life stands out now. My father lived in Cowdenbeath all his days, until he died in his own bed at the age of 82. He worked all his life in the same job. He was married to the same woman and supported the same football team. (On honeymoon in the Hillfoots in 1936, it just so happened that Alloa were at home to Cowdenbeath....) He lived in the same council house all his married life. He survived two world wars, and was not suprised to do so. He attended the same kirk, at a time when the sight of working men at public worship was not something to be marvelled at.

When I was a cub reporter on the staff of the *Cowdenbeath Advertiser and Kelty News* in the late 1950s, that sense of corporate identity was still there, tangible. The seven working mines provided employment for many people in the town. Old miners sat on their hunkers at the street corners, amazed by the new high wages. The National Coal Board, established amidst local rejoicing in 1947, was still seen as as great source of security. Politicians promised increased investment in the mining industry, and more jobs for young miners.

Local sport continued to be important. The dog tracks were crowded. (Working with the local correspondent for all the national newspapers, I used to tip the greyhounds without knowing the first thing about them. I well remember a demented man shouting, "If I could get my hands on the bugger who tipped the dugs in the *Evening News* I'd strangle him." In that moment I recognised that while it was not necessary to lie, there was a case for declining to volunteer information which might lead to the wasting of one's health).

Football was still pre-eminent, though its position was beginning to be eroded – not by wicked external forces, but by the miners' better working hours and general prosperity. Newspapers still gave considerable space to Second Division matches – there were only two divisions then – and I would report the Cowdenbeath games for several Sunday papers, carefully tailoring the style for each. (Is this how the first three Gospels were written – the local Palestinian correspondent varying the details for each local readership, with a heavyweight 'thinkpiece' for the weekend supplement providing the Fourth?)

Nowadays, there is no sound of grinding pit wheels. Cowdenbeath is a mining community in memory only. The stories of struggle and imprisonment seem very distant. The days when Jennie Lee walked the burning pavements on behalf of the Independent Labour Party, or when Cowdenbeath provided the Communist leadership of the Scottish NUM, are relegated to folk lore (though local boys Harry Ewing and Dennis Canavan have provided parliamentary echoes in recent times, and Nobel Peace Prize winner Sir James Black, discoverer of the beta blocker and the ulcer pill, still speaks with coal dust in his voice).

And prospects are vastly different. My father's grandchildren don't expect to live in the same community all their lives, nor work at the same job. The struggle is to get a job at all. If there is to be another world war, they don't expect to survive it. Relationships become more and more provisional, disposable. And the Church? Forget it.

There is no point in romanticising that old West Fife mining culture. It had its dark side. It was a culture in which women knew their place – a very vigorous and responsible place, but one defined for them by the patriarchs. Nor should the loss of the pits necessarily be lamented. The men hunkered down at the street corners were coughing – suffering from terrible lung disease caused by the inhalation of too much coal dust; and the one thing they hoped for above all else was that their sons would not have to spend most of their daylight hours crouched in darkness in the bowels of the earth. Not for them the chattering classes' romantic talk about miners being 'the salt of the earth'. They were proud of their boys when they graduated with honours in computer studies, and made salaries they could only dream about. With at least one scarred lung they cheered the prospective ending of the mining culture.

And yet....

Until recently, my own family lived in the shadow of Ibrox stadium, that great shrine of historic rancid Protestantism, home of a club with an awesome tradition and the cancer of religious bigotry gnawing at its vitals (though Graeme Souness, perfectly cast in the pantomime of many people's minds as the Evil Villain, did more to undermine tribal religious certainties in the West of Scotland by the sensational and impudent coup of signing Maurice Johnston than the well-meaning but impotent words of many a virtuous Moderator or Archbishop). Rangers have spent many millions of pounds in re-establishing their pre-eminence in Scottish football, undergirding dreams and illusions with hype and financial cunning.

Of course my two boys, attending Ibrox primary school, placarding McEwan's Lager on their chests, professed to be Rangers supporters. But they were double agents, the only two young fans in Govan of what was officially the worst-supported league team in Britain. As forty-five thousand Huns chanted in busload upon busload in the direction of Ibrox, Neil and Alasdair formed with myself the Cowdenbeath travelling support, heading in one car towards West Fife. Living beside one of the finest new stadiums in Europe, the boys found their loyalties oddly rooted in a terracing which had many more weeds than paying customers. When Alasdair celebrated his tenth birthday, his burning desire was to lead out the Cowdenbeath team against Brechin City. The Cowdenbeath chairman invited the whole family through for lunch; Alasdair put on the coveted strip and took part in the shooting-in before the game. He tossed the coin to start the match. Afterwards, the referee, Mike McGinley of Clydebank, gave him £1 for being his 'helper'. (Cowdenbeath lost 2-0). There is sentiment in the old game still.

Football in Cowdenbeath is now played in a ghostly atmosphere. Often not many more than two hundred spectators huddle in a ground whose broken terraces are full of eerie echoes of a tempestuous and passionate past with more than its share of moments of glory. The old jokes have come true. Ring ring. Is that Cowdenbeath Football Club? When does the game begin? Answer: When can you come? The crowds are so sparse that before the game they announce over the tannoy the names of the fans to the players instead of the other way around. And so on.

The delapidated stadium echoes with the shouts of the players – a mixture of experienced men on the way down, and teenage hopefuls with upwardly mobile fantasies. Any one of these youngsters who makes the grade will have to be sold to the highest bidder. That sale will keep the club alive for another season. What price Hooky Leonard now?

Clubs like Cowdenbeath, which have faced extinction several times, may not last too much longer. These twilight teams with a once-great past are regarded as a dragging anchor on the Scottish football ship of state. There are those who would like to cut them loose.

Are they simply past their sell-by date, relics of a once-glorious past? Are they only sad little dream factories for the economically disaffected? A few years ago, an elegant young defender showed up shyly in the Scotland squad, and nervously played his first practice game with the Scottish internationalists. Arsenal's Charlie Nicholas, bemused by a class act he had never seen before, looked up to the skies and asked: "Where has this guy come from?"

No, Craig Levein had not dropped from heaven. He had come from Cowdenbeath. He had learned his trade at Central Park. Hearts had come in for him with a £35,000 bid and Cowdenbeath, desperate for cash as usual, accepted with alacrity. The club's future was assured – yet again – for a season or two. Now he was worth £2 million (which is why I found myself accosting Hearts chairman Wallace Mercer in the directors' box at a Hearts v. Cowdenbeath Scottish cup tie – Hearts won 3-0 – and suggesting that he give poor wee Cowdenbeath some more money. He simply smiled the smile of a man who knows he has done a good bit of business). Mr Mercer is more concerned with Super Leagues than with strugglers, but if the Cowdenbeaths and the East Fifes and the Raith Rovers go to the wall, we will lose more than romance. The nurturing grounds of some of the best Scottish footballing talent will disappear: and the communities which support them will be diminished. The centralising economic tendency will be victorious in soccer as elsewhere, and the life of the marginalised communities, which make up the Scottish identity as much as the big cities do, will ebb away.

Myths and dreams and pies and bovril may not mean much to the sophisticates who crowd into the hospitality lounges of the big clubs several minutes before the half-time whistle has even gone; but if the wee clubs are squeezed out, more than football will suffer. Football is a commercial enterprise (and the fate of Third Lanark proves the folly of those who suggest otherwise), but it is not just a commercial enterprise. It is about tradition and identity.

And about impossible possibilities. Can anything good come out of Cowdenbeath any more? Can it be that that that promising young Cowdenbeath lad over there will be another elegant Craig Levein and bring glory to a town starved of glory? Will that young skelf mature to be another swaggering, gloriously gifted Jim Baxter who will send the English homeward tae think again? Is

17

this stocky new boy a potential Aly Venters who will also move from Cowdenbeath to Rangers and Scotland and by his transfer keep Cowden alive for another season or two? And that lad playing keepy-uppy: does he not remind you of Hooky Leonard?

Hooky Who did you say?

Dream on.

Who are the people who sustain the club against all the odds, as if strangely compelled to keep alive a folk memory which must not be allowed to fade without a struggle to the death? Who are the people who keep on proving every week the existence of Cowdenbeath, at least on the world's football coupons? They have hoped against hope, apparently against the evidence of their senses and their own experience, that the team they call 'The Blue Brazil' will win promotion to the First Division. Again. After all these years.

And now, that elusive dream seems to be within touching distance. Promotion for the first time in 22 years is a possibility. The glory days may be here again. All that stands between the poorly-supported cult team with the coolest nickname in British football and the First Division is one game against Alloa Athletic.

Can the Blue Brazil do it again, even though the Black Diamonds have long since run out? Can there be one last glorious hurrah?

Or will they falter at the last hurdle – yet again?

May

If at first you don't succeed,
Pull the blankets owe'r your heid
– Iain Baxter, Cowdenbeath

Bremner has had more early baths than a miner on
night shift. – The Daily Record.

D-DAY HAS arrived, and the strain shows on John Brownlie's
face. If Cowdenbeath can draw at Alloa today, the final game of
the 1991-92 season, they will be promoted. If they lose, Alloa will
go up, and the Fife side will stay in the Second Division.

The last month has been a nerve-wracking time. At the beginning of April, the stand – including new seating, new external
cladding, dressing rooms, manager's office and board room –
burned down. ("The thieves were searching for the trophy room,
and when they found there wasn't one, they burned the place
down," was the comment on the Saints and Greavsie Show).
Cowdenbeath, who had been top of the Second Division for
several weeks, were beaten by Dumbarton and slipped down to
third place behind Dumbarton and Alloa. Recovery the following
week against Queen of the South – with Alloa only managing a
draw against East Fife – put Cowden back in second place, and
needing only one point at Alloa to go up.

To go to your chief rivals' ground needing to wrest a crucial
point from them, when victory for your opponents will gain them
promotion over you, has to be a difficult task. Brownlie had
predicted this scenario a few weeks ago, adding, "It won't do my
nerves any good." The nerves are not helped by the memory of
last May, when Cowden lost out on promotion by one point on the
last day of the season....

John Brownlie, Cowdenbeath's thirteenth manager in fourteen years, had got his crack at football management thanks to his friendship with his predecessor and former Hibs and Scotland colleague, John Blackley. Blackley had been manager of Hibs: then bad results for the Premier League club had sent him through the revolving door, wounded in his pride. As a Hibs player and Scottish internationalist he had been a favourite with the Easter Road fans, but when Hibs failed to hold their own with their renascent Edinburgh rivals, his days as Hibs' manager were numbered.

Football is as much a disease as a game, a virus which, once it infects the system, destroys all immunity. So when the battered Blackley was given the chance to resurrect his managerial career at Cowdenbeath in October, 1987 he could not refuse.

Blackley was Cowdenbeath's third manager in five months. Joe Craig had been dismissed at the end of the 86-87 season after a commercial dispute (he took the club to an industrial tribunal and accepted an out-of-court settlement); his successor, Dick Campbell, made a disastrous start to the season, gaining only six points from twelve games, and with the club anchored at the bottom of the league, he was shown the door. It had been an unhappy time for the club – there had been boardroom ructions, with accusation and counter-accusation. The club's 'Player of the Year' disco made the national press when star striker Roddy Grant went down injured (presumably crying 'penalty!' automatically), allegedly the victim of a late, late tackle by one of the club's directors.

John Blackley brought a new discipline to the club, and the results improved. He helped keep the bank manager at bay by selling promising players. Cowdenbeath needed at least 1000 supporters through the turnstiles at each match to pay the wages: crowds of not much more than 100 at some home games not only made the Fifers officially the worst-supported senior team in Britain, but put its very existence in jeopardy.

It was this lack of financial security which made John Blackley take up Dundee's offer to become their assistant manager. John Brownlie, his assistant at Cowdenbeath, was appointed his successor.

How had all this football business started anyway?

Football in Scotland owes its origins as a national sport to the major shifts in population in the latter half of the nineteenth century. Families crowded into the cities and towns close to the manufacturing industries, and football appealed to working men as a leisure-time pursuit. The clinching factor in the burgeoning growth of soccer was the granting of Saturday afternoons as free time, and when the development of public transport gave people the means whereby they could travel to matches, football was set to become a form of entertainment for the masses.

The first great Scottish club to be formed was Queen's Park, in 1867. That year saw the first known game between two Scottish sides – a team called Thistle agreeing to travel to Queen's Park to play in a match with twenty players on each side. The letter from the Queen's secretary, Robert Gardner, is illuminating.

"We consider, however, that two hours is quite long enough to play in weather such as the present. We would also suggest that if no goals be got by either side within the first hour, that goals be then exchanged, the ball, of course, to be kicked off from the centre of the field by the side who had the original kick-off, so that boath parties may have the same chance of wind and ground, this we think very fare and can be arranged on the field before the beginning of March. Would you also be good enough to bring your ball with you in case of any breake down, and thus prevent interruptsion. Hoping the weather will favour Thistle and Queens."

As the letter shows, football rules were in a rudimentary state having, in fact, been adapted from what was already happening in England. The Scottish Football Association was formed in 1873, and laws for football were properly formulated – such as the regulation in 1879 which insists that referees "should never appear as a twelfth player in a team, or the coacher of any side." A Scottish league was formed in 1890, by which time a number of Scottish clubs had been formed.

Games attracted big crowds of men – and sometimes women.

"A slovenly looking, petticoated and extremely vulgar section of the crowd had answered to the courteous invitation, Ladies Free," lamented the *Scottish Athletic Journal*. "The language which came from the lips of these ladies was sickening to listen to. The men behaved moderately well and, in respect of them, it may be as well to forgive the fair sex in the hope that in future matches they will stay at home."

The story of football in Cowdenbeath begins in the 1870s, with the development of the Cowdenbeath Coal Company and the influx of lots of men looking for work in the pits. Among them were three prominent Ayrshire families by name of Dougary, Pollock and Ferguson (the writer's grandfather). The formidable Mrs Pollock was the mother of a large number of sons, two of whom were particularly skilful at the game they had learned in Old Cumnock. Mrs Pollock, who ran a second-hand furniture shop, bought the boys a football for thirteen shillings at the Saltmarket while through in Glasgow scouting for furniture. It was the first leather football ever seen in Cowdenbeath. The boys formed their own team, Cowdenbeath Rangers, who played in red, white and blue. With six Pollock boys in the side, they played at Jubilee Park, a pitch on the south side of the village of Cowdenbeath.

The first public mention of Cowdenbeath Rangers is in 1880, when they were reported as drawing 1–1 with Dunfermline United. Another team, Cowdenbeath Thistle, was formed soon afterwards, and it would appear that the two teams merged in 1881, with the Rangers name winning out. In October 1881 a new Cowdenbeath team called Raith Rovers was formed, and both Cowdenbeath clubs helped form the Fifeshire Football Association. The two clubs amalgamated in 1882. According to Fife football historian David Allan, the club named Cowdenbeath actually dates from 1882, though the official centenary is 1881 – the year when Cowdenbeath Rangers and Cowdenbeath Thistle amalgamated.

The original board of directors included John Allan (miner), James Smith (publican), John Finlay (clothier), Andrew Dick (store owner), James Brenigan (publican), James Fortune (licensed grocer), Tom Skelding (miner), Alex Campbell (publican), John Simpson (miner), Hugh Kelso (hotelier), Henry Fisher (newsagent), John Lind (publican), and James Murray (barber).

The infant Cowdenbeath football club struggled financially

right from the start. Rather than being paid, the players paid money to play. The first of what was to prove to be an endless series of financial crises came when they were due to contest a cup tie at Renton. The players pleaded with the station master at Cowdenbeath to give them tickets on the promise of later payment, but he declined. The officials went to Charlie McLean, owner of the Old Inn, but he reminded them they were due him money for the last away game. As the train puffed into the station, the station master relented and let them board. When they eventually got to Renton, they found that the match was off.

In 1887 Cowden reached the fourth round of the Scottish Cup, losing 3-0 at home to Cambuslang Hibs in front of a crowd of 2,000. The following year, they moved to North End Park in the town.

By this time the club played in maroon strips, and when the Fife league was formed, Cowdenbeath, Kirkcaldy United, East Fife, Lochgelly United and Raith Rovers all became members. In season 1891/92 Cowdenbeath fell foul of the League's registration rules and had two points deducted – bringing their points total to minus one! It was the first of several such transgressions over the years. (Of one league at least Cowdenbeath are undisputed British champions – the league of those penalised for reigstration irregularities. The rest of the sorry and painful tale of woe is as follows: 1906/7 two points deducted for playing three unregistered players; 1922/3 two points deducted and £5 fine for similar offence; 1980/1 fined £1800; 1988/9 two points deducted; 1991/92 compelled to replay cup tie and fined £4000).

Cowdenbeath turned professional in 1897. Soon afterwards, the club received its first ever transfer fee, when winger Willie Dryburgh signed for Sheffield Wednesday.

After several seasons of Fife League domination, Cowdenbeath decided to apply for election to the Scottish Football League, and were admitted to the Second Division in 1905. On August 26, 1905 'the Miners', as they were nicknamed, made their debut in the Scottish League at North End Park, Cowdenbeath. They beat Leith Athletic 1-0, and went on to establish a respectable middle-ranking place in the Second Division.

In 1907, Cowden changed to their familiar royal blue jerseys and white shorts. The change of strip coincided with a change in fortunes, and the team ended up near the bottom of the league. In 1909, in the face of substantial debts of £600, a motion was proposed that the club be closed down. It was defeated. It was the first of a series of crises meetings in the town over many years called to save the football club from extinction.

The club badly needed another source of income in order to survive: rescue was at hand in the form of greyhound racing. The greyhound promoters leased the pitch for their sport, and the annual income of £104 kept football alive in Cowdenbeath.

The club's fortunes improved over the next few seasons. In 1911, former Arsenal centre forward Willie Curle scored six goals for Cowdenbeath in a 7-0 victory over Hearts of Beath, and was rewarded with six pounds of sausages from a local butcher! Emboldened by such unusual gestures of support, the Cowdenbeath directors decided to aim for the First Division (there were only two senior divisions then). In 1912, they tied with Dumbarton for election to the First Division – there was no automatic promotion at that time – but the chairman of the League, a director of Partick Thistle, gave his casting vote to his West of Scotland near neighbours. The Cowdenbeath directors were less than pleased.

In season 1913-14, Cowdenbeath beat Dundee Hibs 7-0 to win the Second Division title for the first time. Election again denied them a place in the élite division. The following season, they won the Second Division championship again, after a three-way play-off, but this time the Great War put paid to their hopes of joining the First Division. The Scottish League decided that there should only be one division while the war lasted, and the Second Division clubs decided to set up regional leagues. Cowdenbeath joined the Eastern League.

Since many of their team were on reserved occupations down the mines and therefore did not have to go out to the battlefront, Cowdenbeath had a strong side. They won the Eastern League in 1917, and that same year they moved to Central Park.

After the war, the Scottish League management committee decided to have only one league, extended from 18 to 22 clubs. Cowdenbeath, who had once more won the Eastern League championship, applied for a place in the First Division, but found themselves again tied with a West of Scotland club, this time Albion Rovers. Once again a chairman from the West of Scotland gave a casting vote to a club from the West, and Cowdenbeath had every right to feel aggrieved at what they saw as a conspiracy.

In 1920, the Scottish League turned down a move to re-establish the Second Division, and Cowdenbeath, along with other angry excluded clubs, resigned from the Scottish League and joined the breakaway Central League. As part of a rebel organisation, Cowdenbeath were able to attract new players by paying a signing-on incentive without having to pay a transfer fee. One of those who joined the ranks was former Newcastle and Rangers winger Scott Duncan. Another was local boy Willie Paterson. A son of Sandy Paterson, the Cowdenbeath manager, Willie became one of the most sought-after players in Scotland. He scored 30 goals in 22 games (including five in one match against East Stirling), and was transferred to Derby County for the then huge fee of £3500. He was one of the first of a series of outstanding centre forwards unearthed by Cowdenbeath.

The Scottish League realised their mistake in forcing clubs out into the wilderness, and in 1921 they reinstituted the Second Division. They also brought in, at long last, automatic promotion and relegation for the top two and bottom two clubs. However, in order to even up the numbers, it was agreed that for the new season, one up and three down would apply. After beating Vale of Atholl 9-1 in the first round of the Scottish Cup, Cowdenbeath had a good season, with high hopes of winning the championship and at last achieving the dream of bringing First Division soccer to Central Park. Their free-scoring centre forward, J.R. Smith, who had signed from Kilmarnock, was in superb form, but Cowdenbeath agonisingly finished second – to Alloa! Rangers moved in to entice J.R. Smith to Ibrox. Thus Cowdenbeath F.C. have the distinction of being the only club in the Second Division, since automatic promotion and relegation were introduced, ever to finish second and not be promoted.

In season 1922-23, the new Central Park stand was opened. One hundred and twenty yards long with fourteen tiers of seating, and accomodating 3500 spectators, it was regarded as one of the finest grandstands in the country. The players signed that season included Tewfik Abdullah, an Egyptian inside forward nicknamed "Toothpick", and also "Abe". He received the ultimate honour of having a Cowdenbeath greyhound named after him.

That season Cowdenbeath played St Andrews University in the Scottish Cup. The St Andrews goallie, Jim Brown, bet nine fish suppers that he wouldn't lose more than three goals. The chastened student had to pick the ball out of the net ten times and had to eat his words as his rivals ate his fish and chips.

The greatest signing at this time was undoubtedly Willie Devlin, one of the all-time Cowdenbeath 'greats'. Cowden paid Clyde a club record fee of £700 for him. They did not have long to wait for goals: on his debut he scored in 30 seconds. He went on to be the Second Division's top scorer.

In 1924, Cowdenbeath at last won promotion to the First Division, finishing one point behind champions St Johnstone. Willie Devlin was the Second Division's top scorer with 25 goals. (There were eight players with the Christian name William in that Cowdenbeath side. "Pass it to Willie" must have been a confusing cry at Central Park, which is probably why Toothpick saw so much of the ball).

Promotion was no fluke. Their first term in the First Division proved to be the best season in the Club's history. Cowden finished fifth from the top of the league with 42 points – only two points behind Celtic. Willie Devlin was Scotland's top scorer with 33 goals, one goal ahead of the legendary Hughie Gallacher. The two men who supplied him with the ammunition were Willie Rankin, the former Motherwell inside forward, and Hooky Leonard, he of the elegant ball control.

The regular team in that season was one which all Cowdenbeath fans could recite:

Falconer: Murray and Hopewell; Letham, A. Rankine and Chambers; Pullar, W. Rankin, Devlin, Leonard and Wilson.

At the end of the season, the manager, Jimmy Richardson moved on, and former player Scott Duncan was appointed in his place. Under the shrewd guidance of Duncan, who later managed Manchester City and Ipswich Town, Cowdenbeath stayed in the First Division for ten seasons.

The club established a reputation as an adventurous, free-scoring side. In season 1925-26, Devlin was again Scotland's top scorer with 38 goals, one more than Jimmy McGrory. Cowdenbeath could not afford to hold on to Devlin, and they sold him for the highest bid of £4200, from Huddersfield. (He soon moved to Liverpool, where he become known as "Demon Devlin", and he eventually returned to Scotland, to Tynecastle).

Devlin's replacement, Dave Wright, was top scorer in Scotland the following season, when Cowden finished seventh with 42 points. A highlight of the season was the defeat of Celtic and Rangers on consecutive Saturdays. At the end of the season, Wright, and outstanding full back Bill Murray who was on the brink of international honours, were transferred to Sunderland for a total of £8000 – big money for a provincial club. Murray went on to be manager of Sunderland for many years, and Wright moved on from Sunderland to play for Liverpool.

Cowdenbeath's attacking style – and their uncanny ability to unearth new scoring centre forwards – won them mny admirers throughout Scotland at this time. Duncan Lindsay, who replaced Wright in season 1927-28, scored 31 goals. Six of these were scored in a 12-0 Scottish cup whitewash of St Johnstone, the Fife club's all-time record league and cup victory.

It was not only in attack that Cowdenbeath excelled. As well as the defensive skills of the likes of Bill Murray, the performances of their brilliant young goalkeeper, John Falconer, brought much applause. Signed from the junior ranks in 1921, he was 'tapped' two years later by Celtic, but Cowdenbeath refused to let him go. He appealed to the Scottish League, and at the subsequent hearing, he revealed that Cowdenbeath had paid him illegal signing-on fees. Cowdenbeath were astounded to be fined £1000 for the offence, the largest fine in British football history at that time. The penalty was eventually reduced to £100.

In March 1926, a league match against Hibs in which Falconer saved three penalties was a much talked-of performance. All three penalties came from handball by the same Cowdenbeath defender, full back Davie Hopewell, who presumably underwent forcible amputation after the match. The following year, the keeper was given a benefit match by Cowdenbeath (3-3 with a Rest of Scotland XI), and the following season he was capped by the Scottish League against the Football League at Ibrox. Despite being on the losing side, Falconer had an outstanding match and saved a penalty taken by Dixie Deans. At the end of the season, he turned out at outside left in a match at Pittodrie. In 1928 his career was brought to a premature end when he broke a knee-cap at Tynecastle – though he did play a few games for Celtic in season 1931-32 after the untimely death of John Thomson. The lithe Fife goalkeeper was, of course, one of the legendary heroes of West Fife. He did play a trial for Cowdenbeath, but joined Celtic in 1926. He was capped eight times, and gained two Scottish Cup medals. It was while playing against Rangers in front of 75,000 spectators that Thomson was injured in 1931, and died in Gasgow Victoria Infirmary. The funeral at his home in Cardenden was attended by 30,000 people from all over Scotland, and his grave is still a shrine for football fans.In season 1929-30, Falconer's replacement, Bob Middleton, became the first Cowdenbeath player to play for Scotland, in an international match against Ireland. Duncan Lindsay was Scotland's top scorer with 25 goals, and it was only a matter of time before he was transferred to Newcastle. Willie Devlin made a romantic and popular return to Cowdenbeath after a spell with Liverpool, but the old pace and sharpness had gone and he made little impact second time around. He did, however, make a memorable impression in his last game for the Fifers, scoring twice in a 4-3 victory over Partick Thistle at Firhill. He shared the goals with the other remaining member of the promotion-winning Cowdenbeath side, Willie Pullar, who was also making his last appearance for the club. Devlin was Cowdenbeath's record goalscorer, with 120 league goals to his credit, while Pullar held the club record for league appearances.

Another favourite son who made a prodigal's return to Central Park was Hooky Leonard, after two years in America. He scored six goals in his first eight games, was selected for the Scottish League, and was transferred to Sunderland within two months of his return to Fife. Not long afterwards, Bob Middleton joined Hooky at Sunderland.

Cowdenbeath produced yet another prolific goalscorer, this time in the shape of Jim Paterson, signed from St Johnstone. In two seasons he scored 54 league goals and gained three Scottish caps before his inevitable transfer – to Leicester City.

In September 1930, Cowdenbeath signed young inside forward Alex Venters from the local juvenile side Southend Rovers. After being farmed out as a junior to St Andrews United, he was called up to Central Park and soon established a good understanding with Jim Paterson and winger Willie Stewart. After Paterson's transfer, Venters was the main line of supply for new centre forward Stewart Renfrew, who scored a hat-trick in each of his first three games for Cowdenbeath. In 1933 the Scottish selectors saw the chunky, tough Venters score a brilliant hat-trick against St Johnstone, and picked him to represent Scotland against Ireland. The clubs were queuing up for him, and with bottom-of-the-league Cowdenbeath desperate for cash to pay off debts, it was only a matter of time before he went. Hibs offered £1000 for 'Aly', but the club turned the offer down. A few weeks later Cowdenbeath agreed to sell him to Blackburn Rovers for £2500 – but the player asked for more time to think things over. Bill Struth, manager of Glasgow Rangers made a move for him, and Venters went to Ibrox in exchange for £2500 plus a player. He went on to win many honours for Rangers. In 1939, he ended the season as leading goalscorer in Division One. Aged 26 when the war broke out, he had won two further caps, two Scottish cup winners medals and three league championship medals. During the war he gained four championship medals, four Southern League Cup winners medals and three more international caps.(In 1947, Aly almost returned to Central Park from Third Lanark, but moved instead to Blackburn Rovers, who had so narrowly missed out on signing him in 1933. Blackburn were facing relegation at the time, and in six games Venters led a successful rescue mission. He is regarded by many as the greatest player ever to wear Cowdenbeath colours.

Cowdenbeath had to sell Venters in order to keep the creditors at bay. In 1932, during one of the club's periodic financial crises, a public meeting was called in the Co-operative Hall to discuss the desperate situation.It was agreed to form the Cowdenbeath Supporters Club, with local journalist Bob Holman as chairman. The club paid for more than 100 season tickets the following season, and embarked on fundraising schemes.

Cowdenbeath had lost their manager, Scott Duncan, who had moved to manage Manchester United in 1933. Captain Tom Frame and winger Willie Stewart followed Duncan to Manchester, and full back Tom Russell was transferred to Rangers. (As part of the Manchester transfer deals, Cowdenbeath travelled south to play a friendly against Manchester United. Cowden lost 10-1, with Willie Stewart scoring two goals against his old mates. Neil Dewar from Third Lanark, making his debut, scored five). Cowden simply could not survive the loss of so many good players, and they were relegated in 1934. They had only had five victories in 38 games, conceding 118 goals in the process.

These ten proud years in the First Division represent Cowdenbeath's finest years, the time to which the few surviving very old-timers look back with pride. To be identified with a club which boasted the superb goalkeeping of John Falconer and Bob Middleton, the elegant defensive skills of Bill Murray, Tom Frame and Tom Russell, the entertaining midfield brilliance of Hooky Leonard and Alex Venters, the tricky wing play of Willie Pullar and Willie Stewart, and the scoring ability of Willie Devlin, Dave Wright, Duncan Lindsay, Jim Paterson and Stewart Renfrew was to be a proud man. The pride was increased on the not entirely unpredictable occasions when Rangers and Celtic were successfully ambushed by the skilful Miners. It was a heroic era in the life of a mining community, made possible by the support of a crowd whose ability to pay their way in to Central Park was based on their employment in the coal industry. Crowds of several thousand were not unusual – a cup tie against Motherwell in the late 1920s attracted 18,000 people.

But as the Twenties gave way to the Hungry Thirties, the coal industry suffered, and there was great hardship. The changed economic circumstances had their effect on the football club, which could only survive by transferring its best players. This in turn led to a weakening of the club's playing position, and relegation in 1934 was no surprise. The club was managerless, almost playerless, and broke.

At the club's annual general meeting, the chairman, Bill Hodge, reported that the future of Cowdenbeath FC was again in jeopardy. A special meeting was called to decide if the club should continue in being. It was agreed to continue, and local schoolmaster John Dougary, who applied for the job "as a bit of a joke", agreed to be manager in his spare time on a voluntary basis.

John Dougary is one of the great figures in Cowdenbeath's history. Son of one of the founding fathers of the club, he played for Stoke City before returning to Cowdenbeath to work as a teacher, and to set up local schoolboys' football leagues. His willingness to be unpaid manager of Cowdenbeath Football Club in their hour of need undoubtedly helped save the club yet again. Shortly before the new season started, there was only one signed player, John Wilkie, and the club's bank balance was 9d! Money was raised by selling several players, including Stewart Renfrew, and the players who signed for Cowdenbeath were not even household names in their own households. Ony one win was recorded in the first eleven games, and the club suffered its record home defeat, 10-1 at the hands of St Bernard's.

By November 1934, the club was facing bankruptcy, and the directors came to the rescue again – the chairman putting in £50 and the other directors £25 each. In January 1935, the directors had to bail the club out again, and the desperate financial situation was eased by a cup draw against Rangers. The following year, an extraordinary meeting of the shareholders was told that the club was still in "dire financial straits", mainly through lack of support. Local businessmen were asked to rally round and put money into the club.

In 1937, the directors came to the courageous conclusion that the only way forward was to seek promotion to the First Division again, and win back the crowds. To do that, they needed to unearth yet another prolific goalscorer – and they did. Rab Walls, a centre forward who had played with Hearts and St Bernard's, signed up for a month's trial. He scored four goals in the Fife club's 10-0 rout of Brechin City. He was renowned for his cannonball shot – several times he scored with shots which carried the goalkeeper into the back of the net.

The following season – the players were offered double bonus for wins – started well. They beat Partick Thistle in the first round of the Scottish Cup, and Rab Walls scored six goals in a 7-1 win against Stenhousemuir. In their defeat of St Bernard's at Central Park, Walls scored the club's 100th goal for the second successive season.

Again, their star players attracted attention. Cowdenbeath quickly agreed to an £8000 bid from Arsenal for full-back George Jordan, but the player refused. He walked into John Dougary's office and demanded: "Don't you want me to play for Cowdenbeath? If not, I'll no be playing for anybody else."

With team spirit like this, it was no surprise that Cowdenbeath won the Second Division championship in 1939 with a record 60 points from 34 games (maximum pointage, 68). Rab Walls, Scotland's leading scorer, established a goal-scoring record with 54 goals (including nine hat-tricks) to his credit. Cowden lost only two games in the whole season, and won the title 12 points ahead of Alloa.

The team which won the championship was another which comes easily to the tongue of old Cowdenbeath fans:

Hill; Jordan and Rougvie; Gillies, Rhodi and Hillan; Watters, Milne, Walls, Reid and Boag.

It was not a side with the class of the Twenties promotion-winning team, but it was a good team. In addition to Walls and Jordan, there were some outstanding players. Willie 'Happy Feet' Reid also refused a transfer to Arsenal, and skipper Ralph Rougvie and wingers John Watters and Dickie Boag attracted a great deal of attention.

First Division again?

Not really. Once again, war intervened. Cowdenbeath's season in the top rank lasted only five games.

Cowdenbeath's last game before closure was the first match ever watched at Central Park by eight year old Harry Ewing, later to become a Member of Parliament, latterly Lord Ewing of Kirkford.

"Central Park housed large crowds for all the home games," he told me. "For eight year olds like me at the time, the common thing was to be given a penny by your mother....dad was at the match...and that got you in at half time to see the second half. My abiding memory of that match was of Cowdenbeath right back George Jordan, who was a very strong and cultured player, making his way towards the High Street end which Celtic were defending, and after beating man after man he unleashed a tremendous shot from just outside the penalty box, narrowly missing the goals, and completely shattering a low wooden fence which surrounded the pitch and greyhound track.

"Few, if any, in the big crowd that day realised the drama of the events which would follow within days of that match. George Jordan decided to join the army and fight for his country. Within days he was joined by a number of other players at Central Park, and before the next game was due, Cowdenbeath did not have a team to put on the park. The club could not fulfil its fixtures, and astonishingly were fined £500 by the Scottish League. Willie Reid was sold to St Mirren to pay the fine, and the club closed down for the duration of the war."

That £500 fine still hurts, more than fifty years on.

"When I read of people complaining about the Victorian and bureaucratic attitude of those who administer the game in Scotland," says Harry, "the impression is given that this is a recent development. The experience of Cowdenbeath over fifty years ago shows that it has been one of the worst features of the game in Scotland for very many years. Imagine being fined basically because your players decided to fight for their country! More than fifty years on that still rankles with me, and to this day I think that fine should be returned to the club and the record amended to reflect the true nature of what actually happened."

George Jordan was killed on D-Day plus two. Rab Walls emigrated to Canada.

All that was left were dreams of what might have been....

* * * * * * *

May 2, 1992. New dreams, new nightmares. Can Cowden go ahead of Alloa again, more than fifty years on? Will a Third World War intervene? Where have all the fans come from? Buses and cars, sporting blue and white favours, are seen everywhere on the road from Cowdenbeath to Alloa.

Oddly, Cowdenbeath have become a cult club. Is it the strange name on the football coupons, sounding like Cows and Beef? Is it the focus on the club in the Saints and Greavsie Show, with Jimmy

Greaves wearing the newly-issued Cowdenbeath away strip, which Greaves avers must have been designed by the club directors when they were drunk? This theory is supported by Cowdenbeath fanzine editor, Frank Dillon.

"For the life of me, I don't know why there's all this interest," he says. "Maybe it's our new away strip, which looks like it was designed by someone on magic mushrooms!"

There are sixty paid up members of the Yeovil Cowdenbeath Supporters Club, based on the Railway Hotel bar. How did it begin?

"Local footballers used to come in every night and were always asking for the results of teams like Liverpool and Arsenal," says landlord Alan Crowe. "One day they started coming out with obscure ones and I said 'You'll be asking me next how Cowdenbeath got on!'

"Things snowballed after that, and we decided to travel up from Somerset to Cowdenbeath to watch the last game of the season."

The decision to support Cowdenbeath caused controversy in Paddy Ashdown territory. An exiled Scot, Bob McGhee, from Greenock, refused to appear for the Railway Hotel's darts side if his team mates appeared in Cowdenbeath colours.

"I've warned the lads not to wear their Cowdenbeath colours in front of me, or else," he said. "Maybe if Cowdenbeath make it out of the Second Division I'll go to see them lose to Morton," he said.

There are newly formed supporters clubs in Yorkshire and Liverpool and Orkney, and there's a Cowdenbeath branch in Ireland called "The Cornbeefies". There are supporters in America. Harry Ewing MP is wearing a Cowdenbeath FC tie at Westminster when he is approached by a curious English Tory MP, James Blackburn. That's amazing, says Blackburn: HOOKY LEONARD WAS MY UNCLE! In that immortal phrase, worthy of the title of an exotic West Fife novel, the House of Commons Cowdenbeath Supporters Club is born. Dennis Canavan and Gordon Brown join the ranks, and when one of the House of Commons policemen from West Fife is presented with his Cowdenbeath tie, he breaks down and cries.

One thing is certain on this May day. As many as possible of these supporters are heading out in the Spring sunshine towards a strange Mecca which is not on the lips of the country – Recreation Park, Alloa.

A new chapter of the history of the world is about to be written.

It is seven minutes past three. The start of the game has been delayed to allow more than five thousand fans to settle in the little ground, which has an official capacity of just over four thousand. Two thirds of the supporters wear blue and white. Despite their confident songs, they are nervous. An enormous cheer goes up as the 'Blue Brazil' emerge on to the field. The players are nervous, too. They do not want to contemplate failure; but it has forced its way into their dreams.

In the dugout, John Brownlie tries to appear calm. But there is fear in his eyes.

Why is he doing this?

The season has been a remarkable one. Before a ball was kicked, John Brownlie had to sell his top scorer Allan McKenzie to near-neighbours Raith Rovers for £20,000. Then Brownlie made his only purchase from a senior club (all the others were juniors or free-transfer men), buying Peter Lamont from Clydebank for £7500. Lamont, who had been a free-scoring forward with Alloa before moving to Clydebank for £15,000, arrived at Cowdenbeath needing to lose, in his manager's estimate, more than half a stone in weight. It was an underestimate. The extra pounds never quite went – he was nicknamed "Sumo" by the fans – but Lamont was an immediate hit. His positional sense and ball control made up for his lack of pace – his deceptive, lazy style was not unlike that of Andy Ritchie, the former Celtic and Morton star – and up until the Alloa game he had scored 21 goals. His partner, Graham Buckley, had also recorded 21 goals, the combined tally helping to make Cowdenbeath the fourth highest scorers in the country.

Early in the season Cowden had beaten Arbroath 5-1 in the Scottish Cup – Lamont scoring a hat-trick on his debut – but were promptly fined £4000 and ordered to replay the tie. One of the

Cowdenbeath players was not properly registered, the fifth time this had happened in the club's history. Cowdenbeath also lost the services of the talented David Taylor, who had to give up the game on medical advice following serious cruciate ligament injury. Taylor had been a B & Q Skills Award winner and had been expected to move on for a fee in excess of £70,000.

The second half of the season had seen Cowdenbeath gain 27 points from 19 games, ensuring that the Fife club were seldom out of the top four. Manager Brownlie had been able to play a settled team for most of the season, with full backs Davie Watt and Sandy Robertson playing 36 games, centre half Eric Archibald making 35 appearances, and midfielder Gus Malone making 30 starts. Captain Neil Irvine had played 28 times, with sweeper Dave McGovern (27), goalkeeper Willie Lamont (25) and midfielder John Wright (24).

On the morning of the vital match, Graham Buckley has risen as usual at five o'clock in the morning to do his round as a postman. Like the other players, he is nervous as the referee sets off the promotion battle. The early play is scrappy, with nerves evident. Lamont goes close with a snap shot, then Malone and Scott test the home keeper. In the tenth minute, O'Hanlon in the Cowdenbeath goal is beaten, but the ball rebounds from the crossbar.

Half time: 0-0

The second half is just as scrappy, with both sets of players fearful of making a mistake. With ten minutes to go, the desperate Alloa players pump high balls into the Cowdenbeath goal area. The Cowdenbeath defence stands firm.

Then, with seconds left, a teasing ball is fired across the visiting penalty area, and for once the Cowden defenders are absent without leave. With two Alloa forwards moving in to score the goal which will give them promotion, O'Hanlon dives to stop the ball on the goal line.

The whistle blows. Cowdenbeath are in the First Division for the first time in 22 years, with 51 points to their credit – one less than champions Dumbarton.

Cowdenbeath team: O'Hanlon, Watt, Robertson; Irvine,

Archibald, McGovern; Wright, Malone, Lamont, Buckley, Scott.

The Cowdenbeath fans pour on to the pitch, dancing and singing, while the players join in the singing from a balcony draped with a Blue Brazil banner. Then back to the dressing room for champagne. John Brownlie's name is chanted by the Cowdenbeath supporters, who refuse to leave the ground, and he comes out on the balcony to take his bow. Choked with emotion, he says hoarsely: "I can't thank the supporters enough for their backing. Even when we were up against it they cheered our every move, and it was a marvellous experience. I don't know where all these people came from, but we've got to try to ensure that they continue to follow us next season.

"Now that we are up we must attempt to stimulate greater interest in the club among the local community. Let's hope we can give the supporters even more to cheer about next season."

Within a month, John Brownlie was reluctantly walking out of Central Park for the last time as manager, leaving behind him a team which refused to sign on for the new season, and a disaffected and disillusioned support.

Cowdenbeath would once again in their history be managerless, playerless, and almost broke.

Gordon McDougall, Cowdenbeath chairman, in the wreckage of the burnt-out stand.

June

There are two tragedies in life. One is not to get your heart's desire. The other is to get it.
– George Bernard Shaw.

How did Cowdenbeath get the nickname 'The Blue Brazil'? Easy. Cowden play in blue and have the same debt as a Third World country – Big Bob, Cowdenbeath, 1992.

GORDON McDOUGALL sits in the burnt-out wreckage of the old Cowdenbeath stand, wondering what possessed him to become chairman of a Second Division football club.

The view at Central Park is not a prepossessing one. The stadium has had a delapidated, run-down, desolate look for years. It has been described in *Only the Lonely,* the Airdrie supporters' fanzine, in the following unflattering terms:

"Central Park bears the hallmark of yesteryear, and the ground has something of a postwar/early 50s look about it. The stand is absolutely superb and a marvellous example of football ground architecture. I urge you to sit in this decaying construction before it fails to meet safety regulations and/or the bulldozers move in.

"If the stand is first class, the terracing is absolutely captivating. It spreads out in front of you like a Roman amphitheatre and is similar in style to the late, great Cathkin Park. It may not be that easy on the eye (the weeds and obtrusive wall see to that) but it just cries out for a huge crowd.

"When I visited I had to walk through a carnival. Passing mean-looking adolescents and coconut shies brought an air of surrealism to the visit, and an atmosphere not unlike those evoked in Ray Bradbury short stories. As I strode past the dodgems and waltzers, the ground appeared before me, at once foreboding and compellingly attractive. The sign at the ground declaring 'Spectators enter at their own risk' and the climb to the top of the bowl had me covered in goose pimples. Central Park: scary, original, intrinsically Scottish and unutterably wonderful!"

See Airdrie? See Surrealism? See Bradbury?

The 47-year-old boyish-looking Cowdenbeath chairman does not have literary illusions on his mind. His club has just won promotion, but his board of directors is wracked with dissension, the finances are rocky and there is trouble ahead.

How did he get into running a football club? A Hibs supporter from childhood and a former champion stock car racing driver, McDougall had worked with the Spedeworth company at Central Park from 1965. In 1981 he left to start his own stock car enterprise in Newtongrange, forming Gordon McDougall Promotions Limited. He returned to Central Park in 1989, renting the stadium for an annual sum of £30,000. It was shortly after this that he joined the board of directors of Cowdenbeath Football Club at the invitation of the then chairman, Tom Currie. What had begun as an amicable arrangement soon degenerated into a bitter rivalry which has come close to destroying the club. The real story has never been told.

Tom Currie is a self-made businessman from Grangemouth who heads up TC Oil Tools, an Aberdeenshire-based firm which specialises in producing equipment for the oil industry. While on holiday in Tenerife he had met John Clark, then manager of Cowdenbeath. Told about Cowdenbeath's financial difficulties, Currie had agreed that his firm should act as a sponsor for Cowdenbeath. From then on he became more deeply involved, eventually becoming chairman of the club in 1987.

The club was difficult to manage, and Tom Currie found it hard to give the necessary time to its affairs. Running a Fife club from Stonehaven proved to be no easy matter. He found it was taking up more and more of his time, and was costing him a lot in terms of lost business hours. Also, the club was deeply in debt. There were discussions about moving to Glenrothes, and also about selling the ground to a supermarket chain and building a new stadium. In 1989, an Edinburgh firm of solicitors wrote to Currie saying they represented an individual wishing to purchase the club. The letter goes on: "Our client is motivated purely by his interest in the game, and not by any thoughts of property speculation." The Cowdenbeath board were definitely interested, and Currie was authorised to meet with the solicitors. It turned out that their client was Dublin City Football Club! The Irish club wished to get a toehold in Scottish football, and their strategy was to buy a vulnerable Scottish outfit. So keen were they to gain an entrée into Scottish football, they were willing to pay all the expenses of the Second Division clubs who would travel to Dublin to play.

Tom Currie sent them packing. The board also turned down approaches from a property developer who wanted to build houses on the sacred ground. So Currie went back to running a club which was heavily in debt, and which was wracked by boardroom intrigue. Also, some of the supporters were shouting for the head of manager John Brownlie (it is interesting to note this in the light of later events).

How bad was the intrigue? A memo addressed by Tom Currie to all the directors, and dated September 3, 1990, is in the following blunt terms:

It appears that the whisky bottle was out on Saturday, followed closely by the long knives. One of the complaints was no agenda for the meeting, and that I would not know how to run a board meeting.

Well, look out – because if I don't get resignations, there are going to be two – myself and John Marshall (vice chairman).

It is minuted that drink has to be controlled. On Saturday it was evident that it ruled the day. I have already had two games ruined and there will not be a third.

The agenda will include: the verbal abuse at the game, and particularly on the return bus journey: past minutes regarding excessive drinking: the accusations about Brownlie/Currie old pals act, plus the rest: three cheques bounced by the bank because someone mouthed off that we were moving.

There were other bizarre events offstage. A club official was said to have run his car off a main road and abandoned the vehicle with confidential club documents and players' contracts in the boot. Some of the documents allegedly disappeared, and the club were officially rebuked by the Scottish League. By any standards,

41

these were extraordinary behind-the-scenes events in the life of a small Scottish football club.

By this time Gordon McDougall had been co-opted on to the board, at the invitation of Tom Currie. He was there because of the importance of stock car racing to Cowdenbeath FC, the crucial nature of which is emphasised in a fax sent in May 1989 by John Marshall when an agreement with Gordon McDougall Promotions was being negotiated. Part of it reads:

"I must emphasise the importance of a decision on the usage of the track. Failure to agree would, in my opinion, see Cowdenbeath FC liquidated in the near future."

Tom Currie obviously wanted McDougall's commitment and the backing of his resources, and did not at that time see his activities as a rival power base. Within a few months of joining the board, Gordon McDougall, who held no shares in the club, decided to try to gain a major shareholding. In the light of subsequent events it is interesting to note that he was supported in his bid by the vice chairman Eric Mitchell and by Currie himself, who was prepared to sell shares to McDougall on the understanding that the existing board would not be changed. Currie wanted to bring more resources into the club while taking more of a back seat himself, but he did not want to relinquish power.

The football club had been formed as a limited company in 1905, with 1,200 shares of 2/6d being issued. In later years, 4,678 shares worth £1 were issued, the £1 shares carrying four votes as compared to the 2/6d shares carrying one vote. The biggest shareholders were Eric Mitchell (13 per cent), Harry Ewing M.P. (11 per cent) and Tom Currie (10 per cent).

In his letter to the shareholders, offering £15 per £1 share, Gordon McDougall's solicitors stated that Mr McDougall's involvement as a promoter of Racewall at Cowdenbeath had enabled Cowdenbeath Football Club to offer improved facilities to the club's supporters.

"Mr McDougall is committed to improving the facilities even further so as to enable Cowdenbeath FC to offer both spectators and players an environment which is more suited to a longstanding and forward-thinking football club," said the letter, "but no matter how much physical effort Mr McDougall is able to put into such a task and no matter how many hours he is able to devote to such a project, the recurring financial difficulties which Cowdenbeath FC has faced in recent years and is facing now will frustrate any such endeavours.

"Mr McDougall has acknowledged that the present board of directors have committed personal effort and skill during recent years in attempts to keep the club on a relatively even keel financially; such endeavours have required commitment by the directors of a tremendous amount of their time in dealing with the day to day running of the club as well as some of the directors giving interest-free loans to the club. Even so, however, attendance gates have reduced to around 200 at a typical home match. Such extremely low spectator turnout is clear evidence that the club must find other sources of income to supplement football match gate receipts, and Mr McDougall envisages that his presence 'on site' on a daily basis will bring immediate benefits to Cowdenbeath Football Club."

The solicitors' letter said that according to the last audited accounts on April 30, 1990, the club had debts of £239,434. The club was in financial difficulties, and as well as offering £15 per £1 share, Mr McDougall would arrange for the club's indebtedness to be cleared.

"If the restructuring of Cowdenbeath Football Club is to be carried out as quickly as it needs to be carried out in order to save the company from financial disaster and the football club from coming to an end, the shareholders have to decide quickly whether or not they are able and willing to accept the price which Mr McDougall is prepared to offer for the company's shares."

The letter concluded with an assurance: "Mr McDougall has asked us to stress that he is committed to Cowdenbeath Football Club as a club, that he has no intention of changing the nature of the sport played and enjoyed at Central Park. He would urge you to realise that he has already helped the club in many ways, and that he intends to do so to an even greater extent in the future – but first of all the financial difficulties have to be resolved and the company has to be restructured."

It was an offer the Cowdenbeath shareholders found difficult to refuse, and the acceptances started rolling in.

Tom Currie was by now supicious. He sensed that McDougall wanted complete control of the club. He felt that the new man was scaremongering and implying that the club had been badly run. He had begun to doubt McDougall's motives, and suspected that he might be ousted.

"The letter from Mr McDougall's solicitors paints a very black picture of the club," Currie wrote to the shareholders. "I can assure you that if he does not acquire 75 per cent of the shares, the club will not go under, it will in fact give myself and John Marshall the confidence to continue, knowing that we have allowed the shareholders the opportunity to sell their shares.

"There have been discussions with the head office of the Royal Bank of Scotland this week, and they have been kept informed of the bid as it progresses. They see the latest set of accounts in an entirely different light than Mr McDougall's solicitors, and have stated that they see from the accounts that we have in fact turned the club around and will continue to back the club as it presently stands."

Currie wrote to McDougall asking for information in writing about the number of shares he had acquired and also asking for promises in writing "that football would continue beyond the year of your retiral or sell out, either at Central Park or at a purpose-built stadium completely financed by you, that your annual rent will continue to be paid, and that the club will exist independently of your other business interests.

"I now feel at this stage rather disappointed by your bold attitude and the attitude of shareholders who sold out to you so easily. It makes myself and John Marshall wonder what the daily struggle has been for."

Currie clearly no longer trusted McDougall. He was afraid that football would have much less of a priority than stock car racing at Central Park, and indeed might be phased out altogether.

The stage was set for a high noon drama, and it occurred on December 22, 1990. What happened at that meeting eventually had to be resolved in court, and cost Cowdenbeath Football Club a lot of money it could ill afford to lose.

The meeting had been called by Tom Currie in order to establish whether Gordon McDougall had gained control of the club. It was attended by Tom Currie, John Marshall and Eric Mitchell, with Gordon McDougall and Willie Scott present as co-opted directors. Ronald Fairbairn was present for part of the meeting as company secretary. The friction between Currie and McDougall was evident in what proved to be an acrimonious meeting. There are various versions of what happened, but some facts seem clear. McDougall intimated that he had promises of the sale of shares amounting to the required 75 per cent controlling figure. In the course of the meeting, he indicated that he would find it difficult to work with certain board members, and the position of the manager, John Brownlie, was also questioned. The meeting ended in disorder with Tom Currie, John Marshall, and a third director, Willie Scott, walking out. A statement was issued in the following terms: "After a board meeting at Central Park, Cowdenbeath, chairman Tom Currie and vice chairman John Marshall resigned. Mr Willie Scott, who recently joined the board, felt he should also resign. All three left with no animosity, and wished the club every success and offered their help and support if ever required." It was also announced that Gordon McDougall had succeeded in his bid to take control of the club.

Whether the three men resigned verbally or not – and this has always been in dispute – the public statement itself is pretty unconvincing. Whatever else went on within the four walls, it was certainly not a harmonious gathering with everybody wishing everyone else all the best.

Alan Hutchison of the *Scotsman* sent the resignation story out, and it was broadcast. He was telephoned by Tom Currie who said that he had not resigned, but had "walked out in disgust". He added, "At this stage neither myself, John Marshall or Willie Scott has officially resigned. That will not happen until Mr McDougall has shown that he has secured the 75 per cent of the shares he needs to gain control."

By January 1991 McDougall had officially gained control of the club, having purchased 3597 £1 shares and 626 25p shares, giving him ownership of 75.4 per cent of the company. He appointed three new directors, Albert Tait, Paul McGlinchey and Ian Fraser, and transferred 50 shares to each of them. He obtained a court interdict preventing Currie, Marshall and Scott from carrying out duties as directors. The three banned men, alleging a series of irregularities in the battle for shares and arguing that all board decisions since that time were illegal, responded with their own petition. The battle went on in the courts for some months. Eric Mitchell attempted to call an extraordinary general meeting of shareholders on September 2, 1991 with a view to voting the three men out. Tom Currie was awarded an interim interdict preventing the meeting happening, arguing successfully that a club which did not recognise a person as a director could not proceed to vote him out. Expenses were awarded in favour of Currie and Marshall.

With proof on the interdict banning the three directors finally fixed for March 3, 1992, an out-of-court settlement was agreed the day before the hearing. In the settlement, Tom Currie and John Marshall acknowledged that Gordon McDougall had validly obtained his shareholding of approximately 73 per cent. Cowdenbeath Football Club acknowledged that Tom Currie, John Marshall and William Scott had resumed their responsibilities as directors with immediate effect. The parties also agreed that Gordon McDougall would remain as chairman of the club.

So: the matter was now resolved. Tom Currie, John Marshall and Willie Scott were back on the board of directors, with Gordon McDougall as chairman. It was not a recipe for harmony.

All this boardroom intrigue, friction and court action was exactly what a small club like Cowdenbeath, struggling for its very survival, did not need. What is astonishing is that in the midst of all the struggle, Cowdenbeath came within a point of winning promotion in season 1990/91, and throughout the 1991/92 season kept themselves well in contention. John Brownlie and his team of free-transfer men and ex-Juniors kept their eye on the ball. They were all desperate for a chance to prove themselves in a higher division.

How did it all go so wrong? How did a manager who had worked for four years to achieve his ambition of leading Cowdenbeath into the First Division come to part company with the club just as the promised land was glimpsed? How did players who had worked equally hard for promotion come to the point of saying that they didn't want to play for Cowdenbeath any more? And how did supporters who had turned up in such numbers for the Alloa game vow that they would never return to Central Park?

The full story behind the decision which shocked Scottish football has never been told. It has always appeared as a totally inexplicable mystery. There is no mystery.

It apparently began innocuously. In the week after the Alloa game, John Brownlie had reflected on prospects for the new season.

"We have some good players," he said, "but I am under no illusion about what awaits us next season. We will face a number of full-time outfits, but I feel we have some of the best part-time players in the country.

"We lack depth, however, and we will need at least four or five new faces to give ourselves a chance of making an impact. As yet, I'm not sure how much money will be made available, but over the next few weeks I will be scanning the lists of available players."

Mr Brownlie also revealed that he was engaged in negotiations with the Cowdenbeath Board over his own terms for the new season.

"Frankly, what I have been offered does not meet my demands, so I will be having more talks with the board. I hope that something can be ironed out over the next couple of weeks."

Interviewed about his view of the new season, chairman Gordon McDougall said that a great deal of behind-the-scenes work would be required before the new season.

"The stand is of greatest concern," he said. "Plans are at the costing stage, and we hope that the local authorities will be sympathetic towards us at the planning process. However, it seems unlikely that the new structure will be ready for the new season.

"There will also be new turnstiles at the west end of the ground and segregation barriers on the terracing. All these measures are going to cost money, and we will be in touch with the Football Trust seeking grants."

The chairman added that negotiations with manager Brownlie, his assistant Gordon Millar and the players over new contracts would soon be taking place.

"Exactly how much money might be available for spending on

players is still unclear. We must ensure that the club continues to be run on a sound financial footing."

Mr McDougall also suggested that the board would be asked to sanction arrangements for a new youth policy, and the setting up of a youth team.

"This is one area I feel is most important," he said. "We need to breed our own players, and such is the level of talent in Fife, we must make a start immediately."

Negotiations on the manager's new contract did not go smoothly. With his existing contract set to expire at the end of May, the directors offered Brownlie a new contract on May 5 on exactly the same terms as before – £100 a week, £10 a week expenses and the use of a company car. No bonus for winning promotion was offered. Brownlie turned the offer down, but asked for fourteen days to think about it.

At the fateful board meeting on May 21, it was reported that the manager had not given his decision. A telephone call was made to Brownlie asking for his comments; the manager requested some incentive payments. The directors discussed the matter further, with the chairman expressing the view that Brownlie was not interested in the financial difficulties facing the club. At the end of the discussion, the directors then voted 3-2 to withdraw the offer of a new contract, and advertise the manager's job. Gordon McDougall, Ian Fraser and Paul McGlinchey voted for the motion, and Eric Mitchell and John Marshall argued that the board should look at the possibility of providing incentives.

McDougall then phoned Brownlie to advise him of the board's decision. The manager accused the board of "stabbing him in the back". John Marshall agreed with Brownlie's interpretation; Marshall himself was accused at the board meeting of having himself previously stabbed Brownlie in the back by trying to have him replaced by Jim Leishman.

The Cowdenbeath public were astonished by the announcement.

"Cowdenbeath FC directors at their meeting on Thursday decided that as an offer of terms given to manager John Brownlie on Tuesday May 5 had not been accepted, the offer was withdrawn and the Board decided not to offer Mr Brownlie a contract for 1992-93," said the official statement. "The position of manager will now be advertised. The board would like to thank Mr Brownlie for his efforts on behalf of the club, and wish him success in the future."

The manager who had just taken Cowdenbeath up to the First Division for the first time in 22 years had been effectively sacked. The reign of the club's longest serving manager in twenty years was over.

The supporters were outraged.

Describing the decision as 'diabolical', Billy Duffy, chairman of the Cowdenbeath Football Supporters' Club went on: "We can't see how you can sack a man who has proved himself. For years we have been known as 'the nearly club' because we never achieved promotion. Now, after twenty-two years in the Second Division, we have won a place in the First Division, and the first thing the board do is sack the manager."

The decision caused bewilderment in the media.

"In most of a lifetime covering football, I cannot readily recall anything like the sacking of John Brownlie," wrote the sports editor of the *Courier*. "The man performed a minor miracle in taking a club that had almost nothing going for it into the second top league in Scotland.

"Unless there is a major change of direction from the boardroom, I can see a scenario where the club drops back into the Second Division again in a very short time, everyone is so disillusioned by this and the other factors that they plummet to the bottom of that division and, within the foreseeable future, there is no Cowdenbeath in senior football.

"Far-fetched? Not half as far-fetched as predicting that John Brownlie would be sacked!"

John Brownlie was bitter.

"While the telephone call came out of the blue, this was not a total surprise to me," he said. "Only three days after we were promoted, I was criticised by the chairman for speaking to the newspapers about the need for new players.

"Look at it this way. I have been working on the same contract for about 30 months, and was not offered any bonus for winning promotion. When I was offered exactly the same terms for next season I knew something was in the air, and I feel that the people of Cowdenbeath should know that I have been stabbed in the back by certain officials of the club."

Mr Brownlie said that he feared for the future of Cowdenbeath football club.

"I have said it before and I will say it again. If Cowdenbeath do not invest in strengthening their squad, they face a barren season in Division One. Albion Rovers' experience of three years ago, when they were relegated very quickly, shows that if you do not invest in players you will not survive in the First Division."

The manager added on a sour note: "It would seem that all I did wrong was to win promotion and ask for money for players to keep us up. Perhaps if I drove a stock car I would have kept my job."

There was further public fury when it was revealed that the decision to sack the manager had been taken by a majority vote, with two directors unable to attend. Albert Tait had been recovering from a heart attack, and Tom Currie had been out of the country on business.

The decision reopened the bitter divisions in the boardroom. Tom Currie, who averred that the sacking of the manager had not been on the agenda of the meeting, said that he would consult his lawyer about court action. He also added: "I will be reviewing my position as a director of Cowdenbeath. I feel that I may find it difficult to work with a board which has sacked a manager who gained promotion for the club for the first time in 20 years."

The Cowdenbeath players were shocked by the news, though there were a few who had never liked Brownlie's personal style. Eleven members of the squad issued a statement in support of the ousted manager.

"The majority of the players feel that sacking the manager after he got us into the First Division was well out of order," said Eric Archibald, "and most of the people in Cowdenbeath feel the same." The players also indicated that the personal terms on offer for the new season were unacceptable, and that they would not sign on for the club.

In effect, in a matter of weeks after jubilantly gaining promotion, Cowdenbeath were facing the prospect of a new season in the

First Division with no manager, no team, and no stand.

So why was Cowdenbeath's most successful manager in years sacked? By offering him the same terms and no bonus, the majority of the board gave the impression that they did not value him. The chairman implied simply that Brownlie did not understand the financial realities of the club, but perhaps there was more to it than that. The declared aim of every Second Division club is to win promotion to the First Division. To offer the successful manager the same terms as he had been working on for two years, and not to give any bonus for achieving, against all the odds, the declared objective of his employers, was to make the manager an offer that any man of dignity was bound to refuse.

Was it the case that the chairman and his own appointees to the board of directors wanted Brownlie out? Could the manager be seen as a victim of the power struggles within the boardroom? Brownlie's position as manager had been queried by McDougall at least as far back as the fateful meeting on December 20, 1990, and, as Currie's memo of September 1990 had shown, there had been complaints about the 'Currie/Brownlie old pals act'. John Brownlie was identified as Currie's man in an increasingly bitter boardroom struggle.

The sacking was a public relations disaster. At a time when new interest and excitement had been generated for the first time in more than twenty years, the removal of John Brownlie was seen as the betrayal of a committed manager. The fans and majority of the players felt that the man who had worked so hard to take the club into the First Division should have been given a chance to lead his side into the new campaign. At a time when Cowdenbeath Football Club should have been selling season tickets in numbers, they were faced with outraged talk of a boycott. Inevitably, John Brownlie would prove to be the spectre at the First Division feast.

As the public debate raged, the club chairman tried to set the record straight and allay fears. Mr McDougall said he was aware that John Brownlie had made several comments about his dismissal in the national press, but he had no wish to be drawn into a slanging match.

"There have been situations behind the scenes where the former manager and the Board have not seen eye to eye," he said.

"This was especially the case on the subject of the club's finances. Perhaps we need a fresh start."

Gordon McDougall, who saw himself as the person who had pulled the club back from the verge of extinction, was bewildered to find himself Cowdenbeath's Public Enemy.

There were two views of Gordon McDougall. He was the Saviour of Cowdenbeath Football Club, or he was the Villain who had a secret plan to finish football in the town and sell off the ground or keep it simply for stock cars.

Which view is correct? Neither: though the evidence can be read both ways. McDougall's conduct of the take-over was heavy-handed to say the least, and the way in which he dealt with the club manager was poor. The boyish impression masks a determination to get things done his way. On the other hand, Cowdenbeath simply could not have survived without another source of income, and stock car racing had kept the club in existence. The facts are that in the promotion-winning season, the average home attendance was a mere 362, bringing in a gate of £848. The gate income for the year was £16,118; the weekly wage bill was over £2000 thanks to winning bonuses (the basic weekly wage was £25, with £60 for a win), leaving a huge shortfall which had to be met from other sources.

When McDougall took the club over, creditors were said to be breathing down the club's neck and bank facilities were stretched to the limit. When fans wanted to know what had happened to the transfer fees from the sale of their favourites Sandy Ross and Allan McKenzie the answer was that the money went towards paying off the interest charges on the club's overdraft. There was also talk of substantial tax liabilities. McDougall made arrangements for the taxes to be paid off at £2000 a month, and used the assets of his stock car company to renegotiate the overdraft as a term loan, repayable over a nine year period on the basis of security offered by the stock car promotion company. The stock car racing provided Cowdenbeath's lifeline, and the only realistic way of securing the football club's future was to marry the two interests in a way which was beneficial to both. The football club would benefit from the financial strength of the stock car racing company, and the stock car promotion would benefit from the national interest which the football activities brought to Central Park.

Gordon McDougall and his wife Lillian also deserve credit for rolling up their sleeves and being prepared to do a lot of the dirty work – bringing in the strips, organising the catering, driving the team bus and helping prepare the pitch before the game. He stands in the tradition of 'hands-on' Cowdenbeath chairmen. McDougall is also surely right to institute a new youth policy at Central Park. The club can only survive by bringing on its own youngsters, as it did in the 1960s when Cowdenbeath Royals produced such players as Bobby Gilfillan, John 'Basher' Murphy, Andy Kinnell, Andy Rolland, Bobby Wilson and Jimmy Robertson.

What seems clear is that the chairman wanted to go into the future with his own man in charge; John Brownlie, seen as the Tom Currie appointee, was not the man he wanted. The inept removal of such a successful manager fuelled the conspiracy theory and dominated what should have been an exciting new season in the First Division. The only surprise is that Gordon McDougall should have been surprised.

Speculation about a new appointment was rife, with Terry Christie, the former Meadowbank Thistle manager, who was known to be admired by Gordon McDougall, as front runner in the pub gossip stakes. The other name most often mentioned was that of Montrose manager Jim Leishman, the former Dunfermline favourite.

When the name of the new manager was announced, it came as a shock.

July

*Lochgelly was Lochgelly
when Cowdenbeath was a pup;*
*Lochgelly will be Lochgelly
when Cowdenbeath is buggered up*
   – ancient Lochgelly couplet.

*Eight hours to work
Eight hours to play
Eight hours to sleep
And eight bob a day* – the miner's dream, 1880s.

COWDENBEATH is not the kind of place which is found in the
travel brochures. Its reputation is a bit like that of Moose Jaw in
Canada, a week in which town was recently offered as booby
prize in a national competition organised by a Californian television station.

The West Fife mining town has a grainy, black, wild-westy
kind of public image. During the explosive growth of
Cowdenbeath early this century, Augustine Birrell, the Member of
Parliament for West Fife, came to his constituency with his legal
agent. He arrived in a cab, and when he passed along the muddy
High Street in Cowdenbeath, he asked his agent where they were.
On being told it was Cowdenbeath, he observed that if he stayed
in a place like that, he would get drunk every night. Which, no
doubt, was Hooky Leonard's excuse.

It was not ever thus. Queen Victoria, for instance, was quite
happy to change horses in Cowdenbeath, and stay at the pleasant
Cowdenbeath Inn. Mary, Queen of Scots was pleased to canter
through from time to time ("Quelle belle champs de fleurs," she
shouted excitedly as she contemplated a field of beautiful flowers
not far from Cowdenbeath. The place became known thereafter as

Jamphlars, a piece of linguistic reductionism which dramatically fails to capture the romance of the original).

Scholars are divided as to the origin of the name Cowdenbeath. Some believe that it is derived from two old words which mean 'valley of the birches', while others argue that the word 'beath' means an estate, and that Cowdenbeath was once a small estate owned by a man named Cowden. The first public mention of the place comes in the Blaeu's map of Fife, published in 1654, which points to 'Cowden Beth'. In the twelfth century, the 'Barony of Beath' belonged to the monastery of Inchcolm. In 1115, Queen Sibilla, wife of Alexander I, bequeathed to Holy Trinity Church, Dunfermline, the farm or mansion of Beath.

In a very early gazetteer, Cowdenbeath was disposed of in two words – 'See Lochgelly'. What calumny! What insult! There has always been rivalry between the two places, as is evidenced in the old couplet at the head of this chapter (the rhyme was clearly written by the one literate man to be found in Lochgelly – could it have been an ancient ancestor of Jim Leishman?) The upstart nature of Lochgelly is seen in the two mail box openings at Lochgelly Post Office – one marked 'Lochgelly' and the other 'the rest of the world'. In the next edition of the gazetteer, Cowdenbeath had an entry to itself: one can only guess at what the editor endured between the two editions.

The area was essentially agricultural in nature, made up of small farming estates. The first Beath church was built in the thirteen century and was a focus for much of the life of the community. By 1790, the records show that the parish of Beath had about 100 families whose livelihood came mainly from the soil. The minister, the Rev James Reid, describes Beath as a small inland parish, about four English miles long and three broad, with the land yielding oats, barley, peas, beans, potatoes and turnips, but no wheat.

"It is believed," he wrote, "that a great deal of wheat might be raised were the ground properly prepared, but the farmers seem to have a prejudice against it. A great proportion of the land is in grass and produces excellent hay and pasture. There are no begging poor here, and only a few pensioners, generally from ten to twelve."

The working of coal in the area goes back at least 700 years. The monks of Dunfermline reported finding "black stanes that burned" and they were given a charter to work coal in the thirteen century. The first miners, though, were mostly ploughmen. Farmers got their own men to dig the coal, and the women gathered it and took it to the surface in creels. The fuel was used for domestic purposes, and was sold around the houses.

Many of the oldest pits belonged to the lairds. As demand grew for fuel that burned longer than logs, some men came to be engaged wholly in digging coal. In the early days, it was not just the mines which belonged to the lairds, but the miners as well. They were serfs. As Robert Holman recorded in his delightful portrait of the Fife mining village of Fordell, stories were passed down of miners being chained to hutches, and of young men being press-ganged into working in the mines. In those early days, it was the 'crap oot', or surface seams, which were worked, the inlet being at the place where the coal 'cropped out', or came to the surface.

The population of Beath parish doubled between 1821 and 1831 – rising from 1252 to 2390 – because of the discovery of rich beds of iron ore at Cowdenbeath. It was when shafts for iron ore were sunk that the discovery of plentiful coal seams was made. What transformed the situation in the mid nineteenth century was not simply the demand for coal, but the technology developed for the mining of iron ore. The new mining techniques allowed coal to be obtained not just on open cast, but from much deeper seams.

Mining villages grew up around the pit shafts, and developed a very distinctive way of life. A young boy would follow his father into the mines, and after a few years would get work at the coal face, usually under the supervision of his father, who taught him the art of 'howking' coal with a pick. He would also be trained by his father in important matters such as roof support and the firing of explosives to loosen the coal. After his training, he would be allocated 'a place of his ain' farther along the coal face.

The 'face' miners were paid by results, and they had to pay the wages of the men who separated the coal from the stones and put it into hutches. They earned about three shillings for a twelve-hour day in the 1860s: miners had a very low status. It was an unhealthy and dangerous existence, and there was no provision for illness or the premature old age which so often afflicted miners. People had to care for each other, and there was many a miner who would 'lie on' for another man – do his own work, then come back to the pit to work more hours for the sick man.

The women of the mining villages stand out in a particularly heroic light, bringing up large families in very small houses and keeping the life of the community going. They got up early to get the 'pieces' made for the men – bread and 'pit butter' (margarine) – who would leave for work at five in the morning. Some of the women worked underground in the pit, and there were occasions when children were actually born down the mine. Sometimes babies were nursed in a recess as the 'waste' near the coal face.

A strong cameraderie was evidenced in the West Fife mining villages, summed up in the word 'neeborliness'. They were all in it together, bonded by the unspoken dread of a pit disaster. The community was strengthened by the gala day 'paraude' with brass band, and by the common rituals surrounding courtship, marriage, birth and death. The young miner would come to an 'understaunin' with a local girl without any proposal ever being made. The first thing that would have to be discussed was whether or not it would be a 'peyin' waddin'. On these occasions guests paid to come to the wedding meal, knowing that they weren't piling up debt for the bride's parents. Sometimes the wedding would be a 'private' one, which was more of a family affair. Robert Holman provides a glimpse into a Fordell wedding:

"Mr Clark, the minister, more affectionately known as 'Paddy Clark' to his knowledge and silent approval, soon made the party feel at ease....he was in his element, for he was a well-known humourist, and the fun was increased by his loud laughter at his own jokes. A slight noise at the door was the announcement that the pies had arrived and a little later they were brought in, to the relief of the various helpers. There were two, one going to the top table and the other to the other table. The best man attended to the first, having previously taken off his coat, and he was asking what each guest wanted, from pie to roast beef and chicken, but out of that pie came all the fare, the excuse for the absence of the chicken being that the hen promised had got better."

Despite the hardship, the miners and their families knew how to enjoy themselves. A favourite occasion was the 'menauge', a social evening often held at New Year time. Robert Holman tells of such an evening at 'Basty Reenie's' (Sebastian Rennie).

"With his wife, they lived in a two-roomed house with a stone floor. During the New Year week the kitchen, with its stone floor, was, as usual, spotlessly clean. The couple invested in a large number of New Year black buns, shortbread, cakes, bottles of whisky and oranges. On a table in the middle of the floor were laid six-sided dice and a dice box. There they spent many happy hours throwing dice, usually a penny a throw."

To say that someone 'could'na run a menauge' was not to compliment that person on his or her organisational ability.

The agricultural and mining scene of Cowdenbeath was transformed by the advent of the new steam age, bringing with it a huge demand for coal. This, combined with the new technology adapted from the iron ore industry which allowed coal to be cut much more speedily, set the stage for the mushrooming growth of a fairly tranquil rural community into the grimy 'Chicago of Fife'.

It was like the gold rush, though this time the colour was black. Black Diamonds. What had been a useful domestic resource became the power which fuelled the new industrial revolution of the renascent, confident Empire. The sleepy West Fife hamlets woke up to find themselves at the centre of a population explosion. And the area needed a new centre and a new name.

At the time when new pits began to be sunk in ever increasing numbers, the area was divided into four districts named after local farms. One part was named Cowdenbeath, after the farm near Central Park, and the others were White Threshes, Foulford and Kirkford. The inhabitants of what was effectively a new town met to decide a name, and the choice narrowed down to Cowdenbeath and White Threshes. The former was chosen. (So it might have been Rangers 5, White Threshes 6. Ach well). In 1890, when the village was about to become a burgh, there was another public debate about the name. Again Cowdenbeath prevailed, this time against Foulford.

Cowdenbeath received burgh status in the Brunton's Hall on

November 24, 1890. A Town Council with nine members was established. It was Bailie Laing who first referred to Cowdenbeath as 'the Chicago of Fife', and, when a new granolithic pavement was completed, said that the busy Cowdenbeath High Street was beginning to resemble Princes Street in Edinburgh! The population of the town jumped from 3,000 to 14,000 in less than twenty years, and the strain on local services became enormous.

Houses had to be built quickly to accommodate the thousands who poured in from the West, and they took the form of 'miners' raws' – row upon row of small 'but and ben' houses with only one door. A near-contemporary account gives a glimpse into living conditions: "There was no coal house, and the coal had to be placed below one of the kitchen beds, and room had to be left for the small keg of gunpowder – the only explosive used in connection with the miner's work and which he had to purchase from his scanty earnings. Water had to be drawn from the street well and stored in two pails in a recess in the wall between the outside and the inside doors. There was very little incentive for cleanliness.

"A bathroom was unthought of, and in below a bed reposed the family wash tub, which was brought out daily after the men had their dinner, and there, in the middle of the kitchen floor, the miners washed themselves to their own discomfort and that of the whole household. The mess that was the result of the daily wash had to be cleaned up, and then followed the laying out to dry in front of the kitchen fire of the miner's wet clothes, so that they would be in a condition to wear for the next day's work."

With an average of five children per household, bedspace was at a premium. If there was more than one miner in the house and the men worked shifts, the pressure on space and on nerves was considerable. When the house was invaded by sickness or fatal accident – as happened only too often – the level of discomfort and distress can hardly be imagined.

That was Cowdenbeath. This century.

The price of the black diamonds was paid regularly in red blood. The hush which fell upon the pithead when disaster struck was truly awesome. Such catastrophes repeatedly produced selfless activity on a heroic scale, and highlighted the solidarity and interdependence of the mining communities.

The Moss Morran disaster of 1901 is part of the folk history of the Fife coalfields. A number of men were working in a section of the No 12 Pit, Donibristle Colliery, when they broke through into a bed of moss and peat. They were trapped by the thousands of tons of the liquid moss which surged upon them, blocking all means of escape. A rescue party broke through, but they, too, were entombed. A second rescue party was formed from among hundreds of volunteers, and they had just sent word to the surface that they had come across some of the men originally trapped when there was another surge of moss and they, too, were cut off. Yet another rescue party was formed, and although some men were found alive, eight lost their lives.

Three of the rescuers – John Sheddon, Robert Law and John Jones – became national heroes. They were given £100 each by Andrew Carnegie, and were presented with inscribed gold watches by the proprietors of the *Daily Telegraph*. Sheddon became a Labour politican, Law went on to play football for Cowdenbeath, and Jones became a well-known evangelist.

For a miner, the willingness to go to the rescue of a doomed colleague was a badge of honour. It was summed up by a contemporary chronicler of the Moss Morran disaster:

"In the formation of a person's character, the environment exerts a powerful influence. This fact is strongly emphasised in the life of the miner and his family. His labour is of a perilous nature, and though his speech and manner may be apt to be rough and ready, the qualities that produce heroes are often conspicuous. A very praiseworthy feature is the willingness with which a miner will risk his life in the hope of saving the life of a fellow-workman. In such unfortunate disasters as Moss Morran, there was no need to call for volunteers to risk their lives to try and save the unfortunate men when a yawning chasm in a treacherous bog was the only entrance. 'Abandon hope, all ye who enter here' seemed to be inscribed around that veritable gate of death. Yet, notwithstanding the fact that experience taught them the great risk, volunteers vied with each other to make a last effort to rescue the imprisoned men. And when all was over and the roll was called, who were found missing? Four of the original volunteers. This action portrays the true miner. Who in their class would not have done likewise?"

Who indeed?

The year is 1957, and the call has gone out yet again for rescuers. The place is the Lindsay Pit, Kelty, and I am there, covering the event for the local and national press. There has been an explosion underground at the Glassee Seam, and some are feared dead. Despite the dangers, a rescue party heads towards the Glassee.

The Lindsay Pit, which produces over 1000 tons of coal per day, employs 790 men underground, and 170 on the surface. A total of 174 men are on duty on that fateful shift. The pit deputy asked one of the men to help tighten the face belt – "the next thing I knew, a man was lying on top of me."

Six of the men at the nearby Myneer face set off to help their colleagues. They see the bodies of three miners. One of the leading rescuers, David Scott, is overcome. His colleagues are forced back by the dust and fumes.

More rescuers go in. Nine corpses are found. An unsmoked cigarette is discovered lying on the ground. The bodies are searched, and three of the dead men are found to be in possession of contraband.

The Inquiry at Dunfermline proves to be a gripping drama. Mr J.O.M. Hunter, QC appears for the National Coal Board. Abe Moffat, president of the Scottish Area of the National Union of Mineworkers, and Alex Moffat, his deputy, both local men, represent the miners. The Coal Board seek to prove negligence by the men, the NUM seek to lay the blame on the management. What they are all agreed on is the level of heroism shown by the rescue party. The inquiry chairman, Sir Harold Roberts, says: "The six men followed the best traditions of the mining industry when they made this gallant attempt to rescue their follow workmen. It is with great regret that I report that when eventually David Scott was recovered, he was dead."

And the chairman's verdict? "After considering the evidence given and the submissions made, I have concluded that firedamp at the face of the unit was ignited by a match struck illegally for

61

the purpose of smoking."
    Dying for a fag.
    But David Scott's name lives on.

* * * * *

July, 1992. Andy Harrow dreams in one of the portakabins which serve as a stadium for Cowdenbeath Football Club, contemplating the season which will begin in five weeks' time.
    Cowdenbeath's fourteenth manager in eighteen years could be forgiven for wondering where to begin. For he has never managed a senior football team in his life, never mind one which has been newly promoted to the First Division.

    At least he has a team. After discussions with the board the players have agreed to sign on for the new season.
    "We have made the players a profit-sharing offer which I would think is unique in Scotland," says Gordon McDougall. "We have estimated that attendances of 1000 next season will see the club break even, so if the gates average above this figure, the players will be guaranteed a share of the profits."
    The directors reckon that an average attendance of 1000 will bring a revenue of £66,000, which will just cover the players' wages. Any extra income will go to pay off the Inland Revenue and the interest on the overdraft.
    For Andrew Harrow, aged 35, becoming manager of Cowdenbeath is a homecoming. It was here, at Central Park, that he began his career as a 16-year-old striker. The precocious

teenager's goal scoring abilities soon attracted the attention of bigger clubs, and he went on to play for Raith Rovers, Luton Town, Aberdeen, Motherwell and East Fife. He proved to be a good senior club player, without making the breakthrough into the international class which his teenage form suggested might be his eventual reward. When his playing career came to an end, he had a spell as reserve team coach with Raith Rovers before going into football management with the successful local junior side Kelty Hearts.

The obvious question was how a young manager who only had a year's experience in junior management would cope in charge of a team in the First Division?

"It may seem an unexpected appointment in many circles," the chairman acknowledges, "but we are sure that Andy can be relied upon to do a good job as manager of Cowdenbeath.

He has a good name in players' circles on both side of the River Forth, and has experience of football at the highest level in Scotland."

The new manager himself is surprised and optimistic.

"The offer of the job came as a complete surprise," he says. "It was nice to be asked, and I had no hesitation in accepting the offer to manage my first senior club."

Appealing to Cowden's new-found support to stick by the team, Mr Harrow adds: "I am under no illusion about the task that lies ahead. I suppose many of the pundits reckon that as a part-time club we are doomed to struggle. That is not my view. If we can build on the team spirit I have heard exists among the Cowden players and build up our organisation in every area then we can make a real fight of it."

The new manager, who had played alongside Colin Scott, John Wright and Eric Archibald during a second spell with Raith Rovers, announces that he plans to take Peter Lamont, Billy Lamont, Andy Irving and Paul Johnston off the transfer list.

"I will be speaking to these players and if they want to play for Cowdenbeath and I think they can help us out, there could be a fresh start for them. But, to be honest, this is a fresh start for all the players – playing in a new division under a new manager."

The club also announces the launch of a new youth policy. The

'Blue Brazilian Summer School' for young players will run through most of July and August, with the star striker Graham Buckley – the Second Division's B & Q Super Skills Award winner – in charge, supported by Andy Harrow and guest coaches Mickey Weir and Keith Wright of Hibs. The club will also field a side in the BP Youth Cup, and will maintain a reserve team.

"This is an area we have neglected for too long," says Gordon McDougall. "There is a lot of untapped talent in Fife and the Lothians, and we are strengthening our scouting staff. We have talked about a youth policy and now we have the beginnings of it. We want more teenage talent on the books, but we are realistic enough to know that it will take time."

Andy Harrow signs two promising 18-year-olds from the Edinburgh Under-Age side Hutchison Vale. Goalkeeper Alan Combe and midfielder Dominico Maratea are each paid a signing on-fee of £200. Combe is a grandson of the former Hibs favourite Bobby Combe. Maratea was born in Brooklyn, son of a Scottish mother and Italian father. The deal the young players are offered is that in the event of a transfer to a bigger club, they will receive 20 per cent of the fee. So a £100,000 transfer fee will give them £20,000. And Andy Harrow can sell them the benefits of signing for Cowdenbeath out of his own experience as a teenage starlet who was given an early first team chance to show what he could do.

"We are delighted to capture these two young prospects," says the manager. "They will be a regular part of our reserve side this coming season, and if they show the promise we think they have, who knows what the future might hold for them."

Cowden's close season games show mixed results. 2-1 defeats by Montrose and Dunfermline, and a 2-0 victory over Vale of Leven give the manager an opportunity to assess his playing resources.

The club prepares for its first game in the First Division for over 20 years – against Clydebank at Central Park.

"Clydebank are renowned for playing good football, so it should be a good game," says Andy Harrow. "We must look to do well at home right from the start of the season, and that includes picking up a result against Clydebank.

"I would like to see a good turn-out of supporters, for the players will respond to encouragement."

The phoney war is over. The traumatic close season is past history. Or is it? Will the team rise to the challenge of playing in a higher division? And will the disaffected supporters turn out?

From an earlier season: Murray, Falconer and Hopewell

August

*Were football abolished, it would bring upon the masses
nothing but misery, depression, sloth, indiscipline and
disorder.* – Lord Birkenhead, 1911.

Football? It's the beautiful game.
– Pele of Brazil (Yellow)

AUGUST 1945. After six years in war-time limbo, Cowdenbeath
Football Club had no manager, no players and no money. Only six
out of fifty shareholders had attended a meeting called to revive
the club. There had been an attempt by the Cowdenbeath Supporters' Club to finance and run a team at Central Park in the war-time
North Eastern league – the directors agreed to place the ground
and stand at their disposal – but the football authorities refused to
allow it, as the only club affiliated to them was Cowdenbeath F.C.
    It now had liabilities of £2000, with no way of meeting the
debts other than selling off the stadium and going finally out of
business.
    A meeting of Cowdenbeath Supporters' Club was called for the
Co-operative Hall, presided over by Bailie Robert Maxwell.
Question: do you want the club to be resurrected? Answer: Yes.
The fans pledged £500, and a deputation was appointed to meet
the Board of Directors. Another public meeting was held at
Central Park, and it was agreed to launch a public appeal to
resurrect the club. Each supporter was asked to contribute £1, on
the reckoning that a fifty per cent response from the normal pre-
war home support of 8,000 would set the club well on its way.
    Eight thousand regular fans!
    Cowdenbeath Football Club was back in business....

    The Cowdenbeath Football Trust was established, and district collectors were appointed. Sufficient money was gathered to pay off the debts, and Cowden were admitted to the Southern League for the Victory Season 1945/6.

Having no signed players, the club appealed for volunteers. The first twenty applications were all from goalkeepers! The club ended up with more than enough players, and with schoolmaster Willie Fotheringham as unpaid manager, Cowdenbeath finished in 10th place.

The following season, the Scottish Leagues were reinstituted. There was heady talk of a Super League of 16 clubs, with no automatic relegation, the places in the league being allocated according to ground capacity. The smaller clubs rebelled, recognising a death knell when they heard one, and the plan was abandoned. So what would take its place? The solution adopted in England was quite simple – reconstitute the leagues as they had been when war broke out. Having won promotion at the beginning of the war, Cowdenbeath had hoped that they would take their rightful place in the top division, but once again they were the victims of what looked suspiciously like West of Scotland football cronyism. Three divisions were established, A, B and C, and much to their chagrin, Cowden were allocated a place in Division B.

Harry Ewing well remembers the sense of letdown.

"Bearing in mind that Cowdenbeath were in the First Division when war broke out, it was natural to assume that we would return to the First Division following the war. That would be to reckon without our 'friends' at the Scottish League. Having been fined because our players left to fight for their country, the club was punished further by being placed in B Division when the leagues were reconstituted. Cowdenbeath, in my experience, have never had any cause to be grateful either to the Scottish League or the SFA."

One of the earliest games at Central Park after the war was against Albion Rovers. Playing at centre half for the Coatbridge side was a young brawny miner by the name of Jock Stein. Big Jock was sent off in the second half. (Was that why he declined Cowdenbeath's invitation to be their manager when he was coaching the Celtic reserves – his first offer of a managerial post?)

By the end of the decade, Cowdenbeath F.C. were again in dire financial trouble, and they had to sell their star striker Jack Jones to the new club Stirling Albion, Dave Shankland to Airdrie and Sammy Shields to Liverpool. Rather than face an angry bank manager each week, the directors appointed George Sweet, manager of the Cowdenbeath branch of the Royal Bank, as their managing secretary. Asking him to run the football team was a novel way of keeping the local bank manager Sweet.

The Cowdenbeath Supporters' Club often bailed the directors out. The supporters erected a brick wall round the pitch and paid for new turnstiles and toilets: and on the social side they welcomed forty members of the Partick Thistle Supporters' Club for a wild night at the Crown Hotel. Did Hooky make it for the reunion?

The years which followed were fairly barren times, with relegation or financial disaster never far away. In 1951 Cowden suffered a record 11-1 defeat at the hands of Clyde, and many players were transferred in order to keep the club solvent. Another prolific goalscorer was unearthed in the shape of Jimmy Inglis, whose 30 league goals in the 1953/54 season included a hat-trick of headed goals in the space of four minutes against the now-defunct Third Lanark.

1954: another financial crisis. The Cowdenbeath Supporters' Club, which had raised more than £5000 since the war, had only managed to raise £100 in 1954. They launched an appeal asking for 1000 fans to contribute 6d per week. The crisis refused to go away, and in 1956 there was yet another make-or-break meeting in the town. A suggestion by John Drummond, Provost of Lochgelly, that the club should be renamed West Fife in order to widen its appeal was turned down – is there no limit to the impudence of Lochgelly men? – but the club's balance sheet proved to the angry supporters that it was only by continually selling players that Cowdenbeath F.C. could continue to exist at all. Chairman Bill Crooks announced that the club needed to generate additional revenue of £2000 a year just to survive. A new supporters' organisation, Cowdenbeath Football Supporters' Association, was formed under the dynamic leadership of Jock Gilliard, and in its first year it raised over £4000 for the beleaguered club. It also built, by voluntary labour, the celebrated 'cow shed' enclosure at the west end of the ground. The CFSA, inspired by Jock Gilliard's infectious enthusiasm, launched a sweepstake which was soon raising £100 a week for the club.

In the midst of their financial problems, Cowdenbeath directors turned again to the man who had bailed them out in 1934, John Dougary. After building a side capable of winning promotion just before the war, he had left the manager's job to concentrate on teaching and schoolboys' football. He was also a part-time scout for Liverpool, and was responsible for the signing of winger Billy Liddell, who went on to play for Scotland. Dougary had resigned his schoolmaster's job in 1951, and had gone off to manage the Welsh club Rhyl. His side, composed mainly of Scots, won the Welsh Cup for the first time in the club's history. He returned to Central Park in 1955, and, despite the lack of resources, within two years he had taken them to within a point of promotion. In 1958 he quit for health reasons, and became secretary-director of the club.

In season 1958/59 television cameras made their first appearance at Central Park – to record Celtic's 8-1 thrashing of the Miners in the Scottish Cup. The following season was the worst ever – finishing bottom of the Second Division (as it was now called) with only 14 points. A total of 124 goals were conceded, only one home league game was won, and the club made a dismal exit from the Scottish Cup at lowly Eyemouth. It was not all bad news, though, since Cowden made the semi-finals of the League Cup for the first time. They played the cupholders Hearts at Easter Road, and local hero Bobby Gilfillan twice hit the post with Hearts leading 4-3. The Edinburgh team went on to win 9-3. Inevitably Gilfillan and John 'Basher' Murphy (who was once booked for ripping the corner flag post out of the turf and hurling it to the ground when a refereeing decision went against him), both of whom had graduated from the Cowdenbeath Royals nursery side, were transferred immediately after the semi final.

The new youth policy proved fruitful. Harry Colville, who became manager in 1960, signed Jimmy Robertson, a 16-year-old winger who went on to play for Scotland, and Bobby Wilson and Andy Rolland who both went on to be capped by the Scottish League. All three, of course, were transferred from Cowdenbeath early in their careers. In 1964, another natural goalscorer, Stan Vincent was transferred to Hibs, and amidst a worsening financial crisis both manager and chairman resigned.

Despite the valiant efforts of the Football Supporters' Association, whose 6000 members had raised £26,000 in five years, gaining Jock Gilliard a directorship, it was obvious that the club could not survive without another source of income. Salvation came this time not from greyhounds but from stock car racing (after attempts at both Speedway and pony trotting). The new chairman, local butcher Charlie Gronbach – renowned throughout Scotland for the quality of his haggises – negotiated a deal with the stock car promotor Roy Cecil. It was to prove a financial lifeline. Former Clyde and Scotland player Archie Robertson became manager, and three years later, when he took over at Clyde, he was succeeded by ex-Cowdenbeath winger Andy Matthew.

Matthew did so well that heady whispers of promotion began to be heard again. After all these years in the wilderness, often facing extinction, could Cowdenbeath resume their rightful place among the élite? Could the glory days return to Central Park, which now had £7000 worth of new floodlights? By this time the Supporters' Association's new social club was giving the club £7000 a year, and Jock Gilliard's volunteers had effected considerable do-it-yourself ground improvements.

In season 1969/70, Cowdenbeath moved quickly to the top of the table, and they remained there until near the end. They stayed close to top team Falkirk, and when they entertained the 'Bairns' at Central Park, more than 10,000 fans watched the game. Falkirk were favourites to win, but it was Cowdenbeath who took the lead. The equaliser was scored by one Andy Roxburgh, later to manage Scotland. Then Alex Ferguson, future manager of Aberdeen and Manchester United, almost put Falkirk ahead with a shot which hit the post. With only three minutes remaining, Cowdenbeath scored a spectacular goal to win the match and go to the top of the league. Falkirk got their revenge in the second last game of the season when, with both teams assured of promotion, they beat Cowdenbeath 2-0 to win the championship. The promotion-winning players were: Wylie, McLaughlan, Jack, Millar,

Kinnell, Moore, Sugden, Dickson, Mullen, Bostock, Ross, Taylor, Sharp, Kennedy. John Dickson was Scotland's leading scorer with 31 league goals.

Would Cowden be good enough to hold their own in the First Division? Would they bring pride to the town? They certainly played well and fought bravely at Falkirk.

It was dream time for Cowdenbeath again.

My father had tears in his eyes in the Falkirk stand beside me.

* * * * *

August 1992. Cowdenbeath are back in their rightful place, after several more financial crises and near-death dramas – back among the semi-élite at least. Will they be good enough to hold their own in the First Division? Will they bring pride to the town?

What pleases the Blue Brazil fans more than anything is the fact that they will soon be playing their Auld Enemy, Dunfermline Athletic. The clubs have been rivals for more than a century, and the battles between the two sides have been the highlights of many a season.

How did the 'Pars' get their nickname? There are many theories, but the most plausible is provided by the Fife football historian David Allan. He cites a court case at Dunfermline Sheriff Court in 1913 concerning a dispute over the lease of North End Park between Cowdenbeath and the Greyhound Racing Company. During the proceedings, Cowdenbeath's lawyer attempted to establish the standing of Cowdenbeath Football Club in the football world. He asked the Cowdenbeath manager, Sandy Paterson, later to manage Dunfermline: "Are you one of the principal teams in the Second Division, and almost on a par with such a team as Dunfermline Athletic?"

Sandy Paterson's reply was curt – "Higher up."

Thus, the Pars. Football power see-sawed between the two Fife centres, with Cowdenbeath well ahead in the late 1920s and early 30s. The big change came in 1960 when Jock Stein – who had turned down Cowdenbeath's invitation to be their manager two years previously – was appointed manager at Dunfermline. He brought a decade of unprecedented success to the East End Park,

71

drawing on the town's much higher population than Cowdenbeath. Dunfermline became undisputedly the pre-eminent team in Fife: definitely 'higher up' than Cowdenbeath. And the Cowden fans did not like it one bit.

When Cowdenbeath were promoted in 1970, their fans were glad to be playing in the same league as Dunfermline again. What was even more pleasing was that in that season they cuffed Dunfermline four times, one of the victories being in the final of the Fife Cup. The Blue Brazil fans were able to chant again, "We are the kings of Fife".

Dunfermline went into a period of decline. By 1983 they were playing in the Second Division before poor crowds. It was then that the 'Lochgelly Messiah', the Poet Laureate of Scottish football, came on the scene.

That larger-than-life character, Jim Leishman, occupies a special place in Fife football folklore, particularly in the torrid relationships between Cowdenbeath and Dunfermline. A miner's son, Jim was born in Lochgelly in 1953. He was a Scout leader at the local Macainsh church, and he played the part of 'Big Jule' in the Kelty Operatic Society's production of *Guys and Dolls*. He signed an 'S' form for Dunfermline Athletic at the age of 14, and in 1976, after several seasons with the club, he signed for Cowdenbeath when Frank Connor was manager at Central Park.

His first game for Cowden at East End park was an extraordinary affair. The Dunfermline fans continually taunted 'Big Leish' with chants of "Reject! Reject", and Jim replied with unambiguous gestures. Big Alan Evans of Dunfermline kicked lumps out of his former team mate, and Jim replied in kind. With 75 minutes gone, Jim grappled with Evans and pulled the Dunfermline man's shorts down – an offence for which he was sent packing by the referee. Never the shy and retiring type, Leishman marked the occasion by kicking in the dressing room door at East End Park before having his early bath.

Jim was coach to Cowdenbeath manager Andy Rolland before moving back to Dunfermline as manager (presumably the phrase 'early doors' was studiously avoided). By this time his full-time employment was as manager of the Cowdenbeath Job Centre, and when he came to Central park for the first time as Dunfermline manager, he was greeted with chants of "Leishman, Leishman, geeza job!" By his energy and infectious commitment, Jim worked wonders for Dunfermline, taking them from the Second Division to the Premier League before eventually being sacked as manager. The Cowdenbeath fans were envious of the success Jim had brought the Auld Enemy, but despite his close connections with the local rivals, Big Jim is a popular figure in Cowdenbeath. He has never forgotten his roots, and is always the first to turn his hand to charity work.

The *Blue Brazilian* fanzine relished the prospect of future battles, with jokes at their neighbours' expense.

Q: What would you call a Dunfermline supporter who goes to
   university?
A: The janitor
Q: What to you call a Dunfermline supporter with a good
   knowledge of football?
A: Unique
Q: What do you call a Dunfermline supporter in a suit?
A: The accused
Did you hear about the Dunfermline supporter who thought
   Hertz Van Hire was a Dutch midfielder?
Did you hear about the Dunfermline supporter who studied for
a week for a urine test?

And so on. The Cowdenbeath fanzine launched a mock appeal for the Pars, called DAFT (Dunfermline Athletic Football Trust). It invited subscribers to pay £10,000 for a prize draw, one prize in which was a limited copy of the collected poems of James Leishman. The fanzine produced a poem purporting to be by Jim:

Help the Pars
keep their stars
Lend a hand
and send ten grand
If you're saft
you'll join the DAFT.

The Blue Brazil banners are unfurled for a new campaign in new and exciting territories. The adrenalin is running through systems starved of success and excitement. Are you watching, Hooky baby? Or Pele, in Brazil: do you understand the full nature of the honour bestowed on you in having Cowdenbeath nicknamed after your great international club?

Brazil: the very name is music in the ears of football lovers, the name of the most exciting side the world has ever seen. Winners of the World Cup three times – that is honour enough. But to do it with such style, such flair! The very names are poetry – Pele, Zagallo, Didi, Vava, Garrincha, Zico, Junior, Leandro, Reinaldo, Rivelino, Jarzhino. And the team: balletic, poetry in motion, Garrincha turning defenders inside out with ease, Junior moving effortlessly from defence to attack, and of course, the majestic, matchless, Pele whose God-given gifts earned him the nickname O Rei in Brazil. The King. No one has played what he calls 'the beautiful game' with quite the majesty of Brazil: they turned the game into a popular dance practised by poor kids on the beaches and in the slums to the rhythm of the samba.

The Blue Brazil! How on earth did West Fife miners get this exotic nickname in the first place? Brushing aside with contempt the suggestion from Dunfermline that the name was picked because Cowdenbeath were a team of nuts dressed in blue, we turn to the *Blue Brazilian* fanzine for authoritative information.

J. R. Zhino of Glenrothes says he believes the nickname derives from before the Second World War when the team was composed mainly of miners. One particular Saturday, after the morning shift, a water pipe burst in the town, preventing the team from having a wash. As a result of this mishap the Cowden team emerged from the dressing room with their skin the colour of coal, much to the ridicule of the away team and their fans. The embarrassment to the Cowden players progressed to anger and frustration, which they channelled into their performance in the form of determination and skill. At the match was a local mining director who had recently returned from a visit to Brazil where he was advising an American mining company. It was on this recent trip that the mining director witnessed the amazing and breath-taking skills of the Brazilian national side. As Cowden were in such

74

splendid form at this match, the director remarked to some friends that "Cowden played like a Blue Brazil". He also said that the weather was so fine and the coal coloured Cowden players displayed such fabulous skills, he "could almost hear the beat of the drums as the samba danced its silky tune around the terracing."

Thank you, Mr Zhino. Are you by any chance the son of Tam Zhino of Jamphlars who changed his name by deid poll to Fan Zhino?

Here is the truth: nobody knows how Cowdenbeath football team got its celebrated nickname, the coolest nickname in British football. One plausible suggestion is that it was thought up by a Fife five-a-side side who had it emblazoned on their strips. Trouble is, no one can produce hard evidence for the existence of this mysterious team. The most likely answer is that the name was thought up by fans on the terracing in the course of a match in which Cowden suddenly turned on the style and found everything going right for them. The chant of "The Blue Brazil" then supplanted the "Silky Blue" mantra which had been heard from time to time.

Come to think of it, say the locals, there are amazing links between Brazil and Cowdenbeath FC. Here are just a few of them:

* both have had players with famous nicknames, eg: Edson Arantes Do Nascimento (Pele) and Peter Lamont (Sumo)
* both have won games at Hampden Park
* both have scored goals against Alan Rough
* Brazil used to have a rain forest; Cowdenbeath used to have a Gordon Forrest
* both have fielded players under the name of Junior
* Brazil is famed for its carnival in Rio; its Scottish equivalent is Cowdenbeath Civic Week
* Brazil's players hone their skills on the beach at Copabaca; Cowdenbeath's players do likewise at Aberdour
* Brazil's Rivelino is renowned for his swerving free kicks; Cowdenbeath's goalkeeper, Billy Lamont, is renowned for his swerving goal kicks
* both have traditional rivals who play in striped jerseys and whom they beat with ease

* Brazil were the first team to win the World Cup three
  times; Cowdenbeath were the first team to win the Fife
  Cup three times
* Ayrton Senna is a famous Brazilian racing driver; Gordon
  McDougall is a famous Cowdenbeath stock car driver
* the famous Brazilian dance, the Samba, was invented
  locally by Sam Ball, who originally hailed from
  Cowdenbeath; he was known locally as Sam Ba', and the
  dance was named after him.
* Graham Buckley once delivered a letter posted in Brazil
  Amazing, eh?

It is dream time for Cowdenbeath again.

No one is weeping in the Cowdenbeath stand this time round,
because it is a burnt-out shell.

On the terracing, Neil and Alasdair Ferguson represent the
Orkney branch of the Cowdenbeath Supporters' Club at the first
game of the new season in the First Division.

August 1, 1992 – Cowdenbeath 3, Clydebank 3

Cowdenbeath field new striker Tom Condie from Kelty Hearts
in place of Peter Lamont, who is not match fit. Paul Johnston is
restored to the left back position.

The opening goal comes in 31 minutes, and it's time for
Cowdenbeath! Sandy Robertson, playing in midfield, thunders a
shot home. Then Clydebank's John Hendry is sent off just before
half time.

Six minutes into the second half, Bankies equalise through
Henderson when the Cowdenbeath defence gets into a tangle.

In 67 minutes, Cowden are in front again, when Robertson runs
on to an Archibald lob and shoots into the net. But six minutes
later, Clydebank equalise through McIntosh.

Cowdenbeath are determined to win the game, and in 77
minutes Robertson completes his hat-trick with a finely struck
shot, 3-2.

Cowden look like beginning their first season in the First
Division with a good win. But in the last minute, the frailties of
the home defence are once again exposed as Clydebank equalise

through Flannigan.

All in all, it's not a bad start to the season, though there are clear question marks about the creaking defence. And the crowd is worryingly low – only 538 fans, a good number of whom are from Clydebank. Where are the 3,000 or so fans from the Alloa game? The Brownlie fiasco has had an undoubted effect.

The game to come on Wednesday is the game the Cowdenbeath fans have been looking forward to for years.

August 5 – Cowdenbeath 2, Dunfermline 5

Ouch!

The Cowdenbeath fans make up a minority of the 2061 crowd.

The home defence looks very slow and vulnerable, and they are quickly made to pay. Dunfermline score twice in the first nine minutes, through Leitch and Robertson. John Wright pulls one back three minutes later, and Davies restores Dunfermline's two goal lead in 30 minutes. Dunfermline have a chance to increase their lead from the penalty spot, but Lamont saves the kick taken by former Cowdenbeath striker Roddy Grant – he of the disco fame.

In the second half, Malone pulls the score back to 3-2 with a well-struck shot, but O'Boyle scores again for Dunfermline, Cowdenbeath's misery is compounded when Billy Lamont is sent off for handling outside the penalty area, and his place is taken by substitute Peter Lamont. Davies scores the fifth for Dunfermline.

As they trudge wearily home, the Cowdenbeath fans decide to save their chants of "We are the Kings of Fife" for another day.

August 8 – Stirling Albion 2, Cowdenbeath 1

Youngster Alan Combe makes his debut in goal in place of suspended Billy Lamont, and young Eddie Petrie comes in for the injured Sandy Robertson.

Cowdenbeath take the lead in 22 minutes, when Tom Condie scores his first goal for the club. But Moore equalises in 67 minutes, and with only five minutes left, Watters scores the winner for Stirling.

Cowdenbeath are bottom of the First Division already.

August 12 – St Mirren 1, Cowdenbeath 0
Cowdenbeath make their exit from the Skol Cup, despite
heroics by young Alan Combe.

August 15 – Hamilton 3, Cowdenbeath 0
Is this really 'the beautiful game' that Pele rhapsodised about?
"This has to be Cowdenbeath's worst performance of the season
to date," reports the *Central Fife Times*. Cramb (2) and Trevor
Smith score without reply, and Eric Archibald is sent off.

August 22 – Cowdenbeath 1, Meadowbank 5
The season has started badly and fallen away. Irvine (3)
Roseburgh and Little score for Meadowbank, and Syme's strike is
Cowdenbeath's only reply.
The crowd is a miserable 329, and the home fans are very
restless indeed.

August 29 – Morton 1, Cowdenbeath 0
Cowdenbeath field new signing Iain Lee from St Johnstone. He
comes valued at £12,000, but no money changes hands. He
represents Cowdenbeath's percentage of the transfer of Roddy
Grant from St Johnstone to Dunfermline. He cannot prevent
Cowdenbeath slumping to another defeat.

Andy Harrow is disappointed by his team's start to the season.
"It is not the young players who are letting us down," he says,
"it is some experienced men who are not pulling their weight."
The Cowdenbeath supporters are furious at what they see as a
humiliating month, and call for the resignation of both chairman
and manager. Gordon McDougall acknowledges that the fans are
still angry at the way John Brownlie was treated.
"As far as the managerial change is concerned, we offered John
Brownlie what we felt the club could afford, and he turned us
down," he says. "Nothing more could be done. We have been
lucky to persuade an enthusiastic young man to take the helm in
Andy Harrow, who is highly respected in Fife football and beyond."
Dealing with the calls of the fans for money to buy players, the

chairman goes on, "We need an average of 1,000 people through the gate at every home game to pay the wages and break even. At present we do not look like achieving that even with the so-called big home matches.

"If the club had not been in such a poor financial state I would not have been in a position to buy the necessary shares to take control. We have improved the situation but money is still tight and my first aim has to be to keep the club in existence. Two years ago Cowdenbeath were in danger of disappearing.

"At present things are much better, but there is limited cash available to spend on players, much though I would like to do it. Put it this way: if we had got four thousand at our match against Meadowbank instead of four hundred I would have been delighted to say to Andy Harrow on Monday morning that there was £10,000 available for the purchase of a new player."

The chairman, stung by criticism that he was only interested in stock car racing and not in football, hits back.

"It annoys me when I hear this accusation. I have been a football fan since a young boy and I have not spent a lot of money and time on the football side at Central Park for nothing. I want to help Cowdenbeath establish itself in Division One on a sound financial footing. I will work hard to achieve this.

"I would like to see this happen overnight, but I know it cannot. I must have patience and I would ask the fans to have patience as well. We all want to win every week, but it takes time to achieve this goal of a successful team in a fine stadium."

It is going to be a long season.

September

This Ross seems to be a sturdy fellow. Rumour has it that he attends to training to a ridiculous degree. A run in the early morning is good for any man, but practising charging against railway wagons is completely out of it.
    – Scottish Athletic Journal, October 20, 1902

*If you were to cut Ming in half like a stick of Blackpool rock he would have **Cowdenbeath** printed round his waist.* – Lord Ewing of Kirkford.

I WAS THERE I was there I was there. I tell you I was there. At Central Park on September 21, 1949, held high by my dad, crammed in with 25,585 other people to see if Cowdenbeath could become the first Second Division side in history to dump the famous Glasgow Rangers out of the Scottish League Cup.

The huge crowd – an all-time record for Central Park, bringing in gate receipts of £1661 – was buzzing with anticipation, because four days previously Cowdenbeath had sensationally beaten one of the greatest-ever Rangers sides 3-2 at Ibrox in the first leg of the quarter final of the cup. The story of how lowly Cowdenbeath had gone into the lions' den and had actually attacked the lions and beaten them had enthralled the football world. ('Rangers get a Thrashing' was the front page heading in Glasgow's *Evening News*. The yellowed, hallowed, scriptures tell me how Rangers took the lead early on at Ibrox, but Cowdenbeath hit back with goals just before and after half time. Desperate Rangers, with great international defenders like George Young and Willie Woodburn pulled all over the place by the lively Cowdenbeath attackers, were flying distress signals. "It was panic stations now, with Rangers one down to the lowly Fifers, and on their own ground." Urged on by a nervous home support, who kept advising

"Give the ball to Waddell", Rangers equalised, to a great corporate sigh of relief. Now the goals would come. But rather than dutifully crumbling, Cowdenbeath impudently struck again to become the first Second Divison side to beat Rangers at Ibrox). It was *Boys' Own Paper* stuff.

But the reckoning was now. Rangers, wounded in their pride, were on their way to West Fife to teach the upstart miners a thing or two, and to make their rightful way into the semi final of the Cup. Cowdenbeath, fired with passion, were in no mood to be intimidated. The match programme for September 21 trumpeted: "Very few in Cowdenbeath and less in Glasgow thought we were able to bring off a win at Ibrox. Football experts outside Cowdenbeath were quite sure in their own minds that Cowdenbeath would return from the game three or four goals down, and one went the length of writing that there was something wrong with the arrangements that made such a one-sided match possible as it was only a waste of time. That is only one side of the picture. Here is the other. A large number at Cowdenbeath took advantage of the extremists who 'shouted' the odds on how Rangers would win by three or four goals, even more, and benefited thereby. A number, even a large number, were confident that if Rangers won it would be by a very small margin. Then we know of at least a score who held the opinion that Rangers would

The team which beat Rangers in the first leg of the quarter final of the League Cup, 1949. L. to r. Hamilton, Durie, Moodie, Holland, Armstrong, Reid; front row: McGurn, Mackie, Dick, Cameron, Menzies

not win at Ibrox: eleven of that number were those who mattered, namely, the Cowdenbeath team.

"That was the spirit of enthusiasm the team took with them on the field on Saturday afternoon and that carried them through. Under these conditions, it was not surprising to see them start the game on the attack. The question of whether or not they would continue with that spirit of determination was soon answered when Rangers were allowed to score an off-side goal so glaringly off-side that the defence allowed them to do so. Had they 'drooped' a little, no one could have blamed them but they resumed with as much determination as ever, casting that unfortunate incident behind them. In a short time they drew level and never again did the Rangers lead.

"At the close, when the referee pointed to the pavilion, it took some seconds before Cowdenbeath realised that they had won. Then Menzies did a few steps of the Scottish reel, and Johnnie Moodie threw his cap in the air before the whole team received the congratulations of their opponents."

Which is why more than twice the population of the town was to be located in Central Park that Wednesday afternoon. And I was there.

The first few minutes produced some nervous stuff, with the crowd on edge. It had been expected that the goals would start to come early on, and this proved to be true. With six minutes on the clock, a goal was scored.....for Cowdenbeath! The unthinkable had happened. Cowdenbeath, far from lying down to take their punishment, had impertinently taken the lead. Fife exploded.

The scorer was local hero Alex Menzies ('Big Ming'). Rangers knew that they were in Fife for a game of football.

Desperate Gers pulled a goal back, but Cowdenbeath were in no mind to buckle. They tackled like tigers, determined to be first to every ball. They were playing for the jersey, urged on by a passionate, partisan crowd. They yielded nothing.

I know, because I was there.

And Cowdenbeath were winning 4-3 on aggregate. And there were only thirteen seconds to go. And Cowdenbeath were on the verge of the most famous victory in Scottish football history.

And I was there.

Only thirteen seconds to go. More than forty years ago. I can still see it in slow motion. Cowden centre forward Frank Armstrong – who had scored two goals at Ibrox in the first leg – is in possession at the Rangers end. The only sound to be heard is the voice of Big Ming, shouting all the way down the park, "Don't try anything clever, Frank. Just kick it down Number Seven pit!" Instead of taking Ming's advice, Frank decides to beat big Geordie Young one more time. It is one time too many. The Scottish international man-mountain wins the ball, and punts it high into the Cowdenbeath goal area. Rutherford beats the home defence for speed for the first time, and heads it into the net.

The referee blows his whistle for the end of the game. Cowdenbeath 4, Rangers 4. Extra time.

Cowdenbeath fight manfully, but the miners' legs are weary against a full-time team with many international players. Inevitably, Sammy Cox nips through to score. It is all over.

Full time aggregate: Cowdenbeath 4, Rangers 5.

I am weeping. My father is weeping. Big, hard miners are weeping.

But I tell you, I was there.

Let me recite the teams:

Cowdenbeath: Moodie, Hamilton and Cameron; Menzies, Holland and Durie; McGurn, Mackie, Armstrong, Reid and Dick.

Rangers: Brown, Young and Shaw; McColl, Woodburn and Cox; Waddell, Findlay, Williamson, Gillick and Rutherford.

Alex Menzies, the man who scored Cowdenbeath's goal that day, typifies more than anyone the Cowdenbeath footballing spirit. Cowdenbeath born and bred, 'Big Ming', epitomised the West Fife grit and passion. As a miner accustomed to dangerous underground work, Ming had no fear in him. Built like a bull, if he was injured in a game the hard-tackling wing half and club captain would invariably wave away the trainer and get stuck in: and on Saturday nights, after the game, Ming would be seen at the Cowdenbeath Palais de Danse, limping, eating a fish supper. The man would make Roy Aitken look effeminate.

Alex started his career with Cowdenbeath Welfare Boys' Club, and played for Kelty St Joseph's and Lochgelly Violet before going senior with Dumbarton in 1947. The following season, he signed for Cowdenbeath, and he was a regular member of the first team for the next seven seasons.

Ming's last season with Cowdenbeath was 1954/55, when the club were struggling to avoid relegation to 'C' Division. He was suspended for failing to turn up to play against Stenhousemuir – he had gone off to Wembley to watch Scotland play England. (Scotland lost, 7-2). Ming came back to lead Cowden to three straight victories and safety in the Second Division. At the end of the season he was given a free transfer instead of a benefit, and he was signed by St Johnstone. He played centre half for the Perth side for two seasons, before going to Stirling Albion and helping them to win the Second Division championship in 1958. In 1960 he had a short time with Alloa before giving up the game.

Ming's performances against Rangers stand out in the memory, but it was against the Auld Enemy, Dunfermline, that he excelled. Ming loved to beat The Pars.

There is one unforgettable New Year's Day derby at Central Park which expresses all there is to say about Alex Menzies. Dunfermline had introduced what was then a completely new concept of playing with two centre-forwards. Their two wingers played in an area about a yard either side of the half way line. The plan was basically simple: every time the Dunfermline defenders got the ball, it was played immediately to one or other of the wingers, who carried the ball as far as they could before passing to one of the strikers. It took a while for the opposition to catch on, and by the time New Year's Day arrived, Dunfermline had played fifteen games without defeat and were top of the league. One Cowdenbeath supporter who was in the crowd that day, Harry Ewing, remembers it vividly.

"Supporters like me attended the game more in hope than expectation," he told me. "Let me say at once that the hope was fulfilled. Some readers may recall that for a number of years Cowdenbeath had a signature tune, namely Cadham Woods, which was always played as the team took the park. On that New Year's Day it was fairly obvious that some of the boys had enjoyed their New Year, because, led by Davie Shankland and Ming, they formed a circle while the music played, and danced what resembled an eightsome reel. It was nothing to the dance they were to lead Dunfermline....by half time Cowden were leading 4-0 and we were all dancing the eightsome reel! The second half had to be an anti-climax and it was. Dunfermline got one goal back and the game finished 4-1 to Cowdenbeath.

"It was an incident near the end of the game that said better than any words of mine all that can be said about Ming. He got injured with about fifteen minutes to play. The stretcher was brought on, Ming was lifted on, and the procession made its way towards the players'

tunnel. Just as it was about to enter the tunnel Ming sat up, jumped off the stretcher, and back on to the park to finish the game. To this day, I can recall the astonishment of the stretcher-bearers left holding an empty stretcher. That was Ming. Cowdenbeath will never see his like again."

SEPTEMBER 1992. The present day 'Ming' of the Cowdenbeath side, centre half and vice-captain Eric Archibald, relaxes at home in Cowdenbeath. Like Alex Menzies, he plays for the jersey with passionate commitment. Like Alex Menzies he is a strong, hard-tackling defender who takes no prisoners. Above all he is, like his worthy predecessor, a life-long Cowdenbeath supporter. And he likes to win.

What has been the greatest moment in his life? I ask him. The answer comes back without a moment's hesitation: winning promotion that day at Alloa.

Eric Archibald, after outings with school teams at Beath High School, played for Hill of Beath Swifts. At the age of 14, as a strapping full back, he played for Inverkeithing Under-18s. After trials with Hearts and Dunfermline, he signed for Cowdenbeath at the age of 17, playing in the reserves alongside Craig Levein. A few months later there was a change of manager, and he was freed. He then played junior football with Hill o' Beath Hawthorn, and at the age of 22 he was signed by Frank Connor, manager of Raith Rovers. He was at Kirkcaldy – alongside Alex Brash, Hamish McAlpine and Cammy Fraser – for two and a half seasons, and he played 31 games for the first team at right back and centre half. Again he was freed, and returned to Hill o' Beath. He had been there only three months when John Brownlie signed him for Cowden. He was delighted to be back where he belonged.

Big Eric was a pivotal part of the team which John Brownlie built. He says: "The Second Division is a battle ground, and we battled hard for each other. I don't think the directors wanted us to go up, but we were determined to make it."

The day at Alloa stands out in Eric's mind as he relives the experience.

"What a day it was! There was a great build-up. The team had lunch at a hotel, and it was tremendous to see the crowds heading for Alloa. When we went out for the warm-up after two o'clock, we could see that a big crowd was building up.

"All the players were nervous. We were all queuing up for the toilet before the game! Then the referee came into the dressing room and told us he was holding up the start of the game to let the crowds in! When we eventually got out on to the pitch, we couldn't believe the atmosphere.

"It wasn't a particularly good game, but we defended well. Graham Buckley ran his heart out up front. We deserved the draw.

"What a party there was at the end! After the game we went back to the Kirkford Tavern in Cowdenbeath, where they laid on a free bar for the players. They also laid on a fantastic spread, and John Brownlie was given a huge bottle of whisky. Winning promotion meant so much to the supporters and to the town."

Eric, who was named by the directors as Cowdenbeath player of the year, talks sadly about the moment when he heard that John

Brownlie had been sacked.

"I was stunned. Various people had fallen out with John Brownlie at different times, but we respected him and what he had achieved. He was right to say that he needed three or four new players for the First Division."

Whatever his personal feelings, though, Eric Archibald will give everything he has got for the club in what is obviously going to be a difficult season.

The unease that the fans feel over the events of the summer and the poor start to the season is powerfully articulated by Jim Purdie, a former secretary of the club. In a letter to the *Central Fife Times,* he spells out the conspiracy theory which is widely held in the town.

"John Brownlie carried out the difficult job of leading the team to the First Division. His sacking was wrong on two counts. Firstly, to be sacked for success is unacceptable. Secondly, if the full board did not meet, and discussions took place when not on an agenda, it must be wrong constitutionally. For a chairman to comment that he got rid of John because he did not get on with him is a sick joke.

"A manager is not hired to get on with the chairman, but to obtain the best results from the team at his disposal, thus gaining success. When the players refused to re-sign, they were reported as accepting agreement based on attendances at Central Park of 1000 spectators. I honestly do not believe that the Board of Directors ever thought that this bonus would have to be paid.

"The excuses coming out of Central Park state that no money is available. It is surely up to the directors to put money on the table to make players at least consider joining the club. The last act, prior to the commencement of the new season, was to appoint a manager with no senior experience because, as stated by the chairman, 'Andy is a local lad'. I take this to mean many people in Cowdenbeath could have applied for the job and been considered.

"What is the future holding for Cowdenbeath FC? Will they be relegated at the end of season 1992-93? Will they be allowed to finish bottom of the Second Division at the end of 1993-94 season? Will the Board of Directors then state that, due to lack of enthusiasm by the Cowdenbeath public, there will be no alternative but to resign from the Scottish League? If this does happen, will the ground be sold, or will it become a stadium for stock cars?"

September 5, 1992. Cowdenbeath 0 Dumbarton 1.
One goal from Gibson is enough to defeat the Fifers. Attendance, 419.

September 12. Ayr United 0, Cowdenbeath 1.
A victory! Cowden battle for every ball, and shock the home side with a goal by Tom Condie in 60 minutes. It seems as if the final whistle will never come, but the Blue Brazil hang on grimly to record their first victory in the First Division.

Is this the turning of the corner the fans have longed for?

September 19. Cowdenbeath 0, Raith Rovers 3.
No.

September 26. Kilmarnock 3, Cowdenbeath 0.
The Cowdenbeath defence is still haemorrhaging. The club looks very lonely at the bottom of the table.

Cowden sign Willie Callaghan from Montrose in exchange for Neil Irvine. The new signing is the son of Willie Callaghan, the former Dunfermline and Scotland player who was brought up in Cowdenbeath and is now in charge of the club's kit. Willie Callaghan junior has the distinction of having been signed four times by Jim Leishman – twice for Dunfermline, also for Inverness Thistle and Montrose.

No question about who will replace Neil Irvine as club captain – Eric Archibald.

Question: Why does the captain of a First Division club prefer to play for a team in the Second Division? Does Neil Irvine know something the rest of us don't?

How long does a season go on for anyway?

September 29. Stenhousemuir 2, Cowdenbeath 4.
Just when all seemed dark....Cowden cuff Second Division

upstarts Stenhousemuir to go into the third round of the B & Q Cup. Willie Callaghan scores, along with Iain Lee, Gus Malone, and Graham Buckley. Nicky Henderson, signed from Raith Rovers with money from the Irvine deal, makes an impressive debut.

Is this the turning of the corner the fans have longed for?

October

The sin of modern capitalism is cynicism: and the sin of socialism is lying – C.F. von Weizsacker.

It's a bit like poker, prime minister. If you aren't prepared to lose, you will never win – Ian MacGregor, chairman of the National Coal Board, to Margaret Thatcher, 1984.

AS A BOY, I used to go to the cinema in Cowdenbeath most Saturdays. The smokey, dank house of dreams seemed always to be packed. Young lovers sat in the back rows, entwined in each other, oblivious of what was happening on screen, so closely enveloped that they had to be unravelled by the usherettes at the end of the show. Old men were there in the blackness, still with their bunnets on, and the air hung heavy with pipe and cigarette smoke.

Makes a change from the pit, doesn't it?

At least it was above ground and without risk of fatal accident, though not without risk of terminal disease. It was a heaving, sweaty house of nostalgia and fantasy, resonating with a persistent off-sceen coughing soundtrack that would have done justice to the outpatients' department of the Dunfermline chest hospital. And when the cinema skailed, you could tell the kind of film it had been by the way people walked. If they came out bowlegged, it was a cowboy film. If they swaggered and spoke in Cowdenbeath-American with a cigarette lolling langorously at the corner of the mouth, it was a gangster story.

But what I remember above all is that every time Winston Churchill appeared on the screen, he was booed.

Whenever the great war hero – by this time prime minister again after a spell of Labour government – showed up on the Pathé News, with familiar bow tie, homburg hat and cigar, he was greeted with streams of boos and shouts of 'war monger'. Sir Winston Churchill was hated by the miners of West Fife. To understand why, it is necessary to know something of the development of mining in Cowdenbeath.

The Cowdenbeath Coal Company was formed during the rapid expansion of the coal industry in the 1870s. It initiated the speedy sinking of new shafts around the town to exploit the reserves of high quality coal. By the time it amalgamated with the Fife Coal Company in 1896, it owned nine collieries in the Cowdenbeath district.

The Fife Coal Company quickly became the largest coalmining enterprise in Britain. By 1911, the Fife Coal Company employed 14,000 people, producing 4.5 million tons of coal each year.

It was destined to shape the whole of the British mining industry. Charles Carlow, who was appointed manager of the company at the age of 23, was a man of tremendous drive and risk-taking innovation. As well as sinking new shafts to deeper levels, he introduced revolutionary coal cutting methods. His nephew, Charles Carlow Reid, became general manager of the Fife Coal Company, and he confirmed Cowdenbeath as the centre of its operations by building its central offices and workshops in the town. The Fife Coal Company's organisation and methods provided the model for similar developments in the UK.

Conditions for miners at the turn of the century were primitive. The men spent their daylight hours in cramped and often dangerous conditions, sometimes lying in pools of water while working the coal face with pick-axes. Not enough attention was paid to safety: the focus was on getting the black diamonds to the surface as quickly as possible. Long hours underground inhaling coal dust was an unhealthy and dangerous way to make a living. There were many fatal accidents. And the wages were poor: mineworkers were near the bottom of the industrial wages league table.

Miners felt themselves to be serfs, as in the old days when men were reputedly chained to the laird's hutches. They were certainly poorly regarded, poorly paid, and poorly treated. In time, the miners banded together to fight for better wages and conditions. In 1910, after two major British coal mining disasters, they gained a fair measure of public support. At Whitehaven in Cumberland, 132 miners lost their lives, while at Preston Pit in Bolton the death toll was no fewer than 320. That same year, a major miners' strike in South Wales led to rioting in the Rhondda Valley which the Glamorgan County police force was unable to control.

As Home Secretary, Winston Churchill put troops on reserve and brought in reinforcements from the Metropolitan Police. More riots occurred, and many of the shops in the town of Tonypandy were wrecked. When the leaders of the Miners' Federation protested to Churchill about his deployment of troops, he replied that he would have no hesitation "after what has occurred to authorise the employment of the military." Thereafter, the cry of 'Tonypandy' was raised against him whenever he spoke at public meetings. Winston Churchill was seen as the public enemy of the miners.

In 1912, there was a strike throughout the Fife coalfields, and this led to the passing of the Minimum Wage Act. During the First World War, the Government took control of the mines in order to ensure high levels of productivity. A national wages agreement was implemented. After the war, the Miners' Federation balloted their members on demands for a thirty per cent wage increase, a six-hour day, and the eventual nationalisation of the mines. The Fife Coal Company announced that miners' wages would be reduced from £5. 0s 10d to £3 17s 11d per week. To take the heat out of the situation, Lloyd George offered to set up a Commission under Lord Sankey to bring forward recommendations for the coal industry. The West Fife miners distrusted the government and wanted to strike immediately, but the Miners' Federation, led by their highly regarded president, Bob Smillie, accepted, on the written understanding that the government would accept the recommendations of the Sankey Commission "in the spirit and the letter".

The Commission recommended a six-hour working day for miners, and joint control of the coal industry. The Government, lobbied hard by the coalowners, went back on their word and rejected the Sankey Commission recommendations. The coalowners announced that the war wages were being withdrawn. The miners had been betrayed.

The Miners' Federation called for strike action, and they were supported by the Enginemen, Boiler and Firemen's Unions. The management manned the pits, and the miners were locked out. The strike spread through the Scottish coalfields.

At Dalbeath Colliery, the manager, William Spalding, was grabbed by the pickets who were going to duck him in the Bleachfield Pond. The police charged the crowds with batons and made several arrests. Extra police were drafted into Cowdenbeath during the night, and they formed a barrier across the High Street. They refused to let pickets past, and street fighting lasted until someone switched off all the lights. Windows were smashed, and property looted. During the night, soldiers were sent into Cowdenbeath and billeted in churches and halls. Many homes were raided by the police, and miners' leaders were arrested. They were tried at Perth, and received sentences of between nine months and a year.

Jennie Lee, grand-daughter of Mick Lee, a well known Fife miners' agent and representative of an outstanding tradition of Christian socialism, remembered the riots near her home in Cowdenbeath.

"All his life," wrote the young woman who was to become an MP and to marry Aneurin Bevan, "in the disputes between colliers and coalowners, my grandfather had been familiar with lies, double-dealing and crude victimisation. Coalowners don't hesitate to bring soldiers and additional police into the mining towns to be used against the miners if they think that, by doing so, they can better gain their ends. My grandfather had seen policemen's batons used against his workmates.

"In 1921, then barely seventeen, I got caught in the middle of Cowdenbeath High Street in a fight between policemen and miners. I was cycling home from Dunfermline library with a bundle of books tied to the back of my bicycle. The pressure of the crowd forced me to dismount. They went surging past me, growling and cursing at the police. I had no room to turn my bicycle, or I would have run too. Still bewildered, I found a line of policemen with drawn batons literally towering over me....there was a free-for-all for a few minutes, then quite suddenly it was all over. I had to walk home the rest of the way for the frame of my

93

bicycle had been twisted in the general mix-up.

"I felt pleased and excited and angry all in one. For me this was a childish adventure without any serious risk. But I did not forget it. Miners, it seemed, when they set out to improve their wages and conditions, had to reckon with the physical forces of the State as well as with the money and influence of the coalowners."

Two local Justices of the Peace were instructed to read the 'Riot Act', but they refused. Mrs Watson, J.P., wrote to the County Clerk: "I find that I cannot conscientiously carry out the duties which are evidently attached to the office of Justice of the Peace. I cannot, for example, forget that my father lost his life in the mines, and that my husband was a miner for twenty years. It would therefore be impossible for me to read the Riot Act in order that miners of Fife, my own class, should be shot down by the Military during an industrial crisis. I therefore resign my position as Justice of the Peace for Fife."

It was a bitter struggle. The coal owners' policy was to starve the miners into submission. Soup kitchens were established throughout the community. The Co-operative Society and local public house societies gave donations to help keep the miners' families going.

The hardship was considerable. One Cowdenbeath miner's daughter, Mary Docherty, recalled how her father killed one of their hens when it became too old to lay.

"The police came to our door and asked if anyone had been trying to sell her beef or had given her beef. My mother said she had no money to buy beef and nobody had given her any. The constable was kept at the door, but he could see into the kitchen. He saw a pot boiling at the side of the door and remarked on it.

"Do you know your pot's boiling, Mrs Docherty?"

"Aye. I want it to boil. That's why I put it on the fire."

"You're surely going to have a feed the day."

"Well, it'll be a change from soup."

"He tried every way to get to know what was in the pot but my mother did not tell him."

After several months, the starving miners were forced to give in and accept the lower wages.

At the General Election of 1922, some miners went to Dundee

to agitate against Churchill and campaign against his re-election. One of the candidates was the Clydeside Communist Willie Gallacher, who was later to become MP for West Fife. When Churchill got up on to his feet to speak at the Caird Hall, he was greeted by a chorus of "Tell me the old, old story". Churchill lost his temper, calling the the miners 'young reptiles'. In the event, Churchill lost his seat, coming fourth, a long way behind the Prohibitionist candidate. Two years later, having switched his allegiance from Liberal to Conservative, he was elected MP for Epping. That same year, he became Chancellor of the Exchequer in Stanley Baldwin's government.

In 1925, the coal owners gave notice that they wanted to end their existing agreement with the miners, and they demanded wage reductions or an increase in working hours. The Miners' Federation leaders at once prepared for a national strike, and sought the support of the TUC. The government decided to continue subsidies to the coal industry while a Commission deliberated on the problems of the coal industry. When the Samuel Commission eventually advocated a reduction in miners' wages, the Miners' Federation responded with the slogan, 'Not a penny off the pay, not a minute on the day'. On May 1, 1926 a General Strike was called in support of the miners, and the pit gates were locked.

As Chancellor of the Exchequer, Churchill wanted the strike broken as quickly as possible. This could only be done, he and Lord Birkenhead argued, by putting the government's case to the nation, and by ensuring that all essential services were maintained. Churchill took responsibility for establishing a national newspaper, the *British Gazette,* which would be published each day while the strike lasted, setting out the Government's case. He himself wrote much of the material, some of which was regarded as intimidatory.

"I have no wish to make threats or use language which would disturb the House or cause bad blood," Churchill told the Commons, "but this I must say: make your minds perfectly clear that if ever you let loose upon us again a general strike, we will loose upon you another *British Gazette."*

The government brought in the troops, and the General Strike collapsed after 12 days. The miners stayed out. Back to starvation, poverty and soup kitchens. In August, the miners' leader A.J. Cook came to Cowdenbeath and addressed a rally of 20,000 people.

Again, the miners were starved out, and returned to work in November, after thirty weeks of hardship. Many miners who had gone on strike were victimised.

Jennie Lee recalls: "After the stoppage there was supposed to be no victimisation. Men were to return to their old jobs. But coal companies never keep their word to colliers unless their employees are strongly enough organised to compel them to do so. Why should coal companies be more scrupulous than governments? In 1921 Bob Smillie was used by the government to break the resistance of the miners. He did not know he was being so used. For Smillie was a great and honourable man. When he made a promise he meant it and stuck to it. Therefore, when Bonar Law sent him a signed letter from 11 Downing Street, promising that the recommendations of the Sankey Commission would be kept in the spirit and in the letter, he believed a great advance for the miners was as good as won.

"The government knew differently. Their pledge had been merely a manoeuvre to divide and disarm the miners until the coal companies, and the government, were in a stronger position to

Mining before the days of power, with pick and shovel

fight them. The same sort of warlike ruthlessness was now practised by the coal companies. They re-employed or blacklisted men entirely as they thought fit. A man blacklisted at his own pit had no chance of being engaged elsewhere."

Families were evicted from their homes because they had no money to pay the rent. The hated evictions and warrant sales at that time are part of the Fife political folklore. When it was known that an eviction was to take place a meeting was called, and while the bailiff and the police were throwing out the furniture, those who had come to the meeting carried it back into the house. There were many arrests and imprisonments. The actions of the government and the coal owners brought disillusionment and bitterness throughout the Scottish coalfields.

Many men were broken, including Jennie Lee's father. She remembers:

"We had fought and we had been beaten. The coal companies now had the whip hand. They were driving home the lessons of defeat. All over the country men were victimised. The unions in most districts were too enfeebled by the long struggle to be able to protect them. Then there was this wonderful alibi – unemployment. Oh no, there was no such thing as victimisation. It was simply that trade was bad and there was not enough work to go round.

"Under cover of that kind of talk – where the unions were weak the coal companies did not even trouble to disguise what they were doing – the fight to break the spirit of a proud people went savagely on. Some miners who were active during the stoppage became permanently unemployed. Others were re-engaged, then, once underground, subject to every conceivable hardship and humiliation.

"Still others were driven into exile. Told quite plainly that they were not wanted, they felt there was nothing else for it but to sell their bits of furniture and migrate, usually to the dominions. There were some sad partings. Some of our closest relatives and friends joined the trek. Not Jews persecuted by Hitler's Germany. One hundred per cent Aryan British colliers driven into exile by one hundred per cent Aryan British coalowners. And all because they thought miners should be paid more than starvation wages and had

97

the courage to say so.

"You can find such family records in every colliery village in the British Isles. Poverty, atrocious working conditions, intimidation, victimisation, exile; yet there was no such thing, I was told, as a class-war. All the polite people said that to talk of such a thing was ignorant hysterics. All the popular papers and famous preachers denied its existence. Then what in God's name, I wanted to know, were they doing to our people?"

The government minister who was most clearly identified, rightly or wrongly, with the policy of trying to teach the miners a lesson was one Winston Spencer Churchill.

And the miners never forgot.

They hated him.

After the failure of the strike, morale in the coalfields was badly affected, and productivity went down, partly due to lack of proper investment in research and development. Pits on the continent surged ahead, and by 1936 Germany and the Netherlands were showing much better productivity figures. Mining conditions were a bit better by this time, with the advent of electrically-driven coal cutters. The coal was bored and blasted, then shovelled on to electrically-driven belts.

When the Second World War broke out, many men left the pits to join the armed forces or to engage in the better-paid munitions work. The country needed increased tonnages of coal for the war effort, and the national government (under the leadership of Winston Churchill) increased the miners' wages, and passed legislation preventing miners leaving the pits. The 'Bevin Boy' scheme also gave conscripts the option of doing their national service in the coal fields.

As the end of the war drew near, the government set up a committee under Charles Reid, with the remit of providing plans for the coal industry at the end of hostilities. The Fife Coal Company manager argued in his report that productivity could not be increased under the existing arrangements. More centralisation was needed, and massive investment was essential.

There are certain ironies in the fact that the Reid Report should have provided such good ammunition for those who had for years advocated the nationalisation of the mines. The general manager of the Fife Coal Company was thought to be the person least likely to make straight the way for such an outcome. When Labour swept to power in the post-war general election, one of their earliest moves was to pass the Coal Mines Nationalisation Act. On January 1, 1947, the mines came under public ownership. Charles Reid, the local man who had opposed the Cowdenbeath miners in most of their bitter struggles over wages and conditions but whose thoughts on the future of the mining industry had been co-opted by the socialist miners' leaders, became director of production in the new National Coal Board.

Arise, Sir Charles, the Miners' Friend.

Miners wept in the streets of Cowdenbeath.

At its best, socialism is a prophetic, passionate, generous creed, which brings longed-for justice for many people. But in its utopian varieties, it has a major flaw.

It does not believe in sin.

Or it locates it simply in the structures of capitalism.

When the Revolution comes, says the utopian version of the creed, there will be harmonious brotherhood and the state will wither away. Such naïvety almost cries out for betrayal. And the betrayal comes not simply from the evil capitalists, but from within its own class.

Socialism is at its most dangerously vulnerable when it has just won a famous victory. The idealism of the Bolshevik revolution was taken over by Stalin, the leader of the working classes who sent millions of the working classes to perish in gulags. Naïve and utopian British socialists, with blinkered eyes focused on the evils of capitalism, rejected even the evidence of their senses in favour of a theory that all good socialists would stand together and that none of their leaders would sell their brothers down the river. They were in a trance: and they condoned betrayal after betrayal after betrayal.

January 1, 1947 was the day many miners had longed for. Their leaders had preached such a vision at the soup kitchens and rallies, and these visions had kept the miners and their families going during times of extreme hardship. At last the kingdom had come and life would be secure. Wages and conditions improved considerably, and the five-day working week was achieved. New mining techniques from the continent heralded the end of the pick-and-shovel method of coal cutting, and new safety regulations meant that the mines were much safer places of work. Disasters were much more likely to happen because of illicit smoking underground than because of external causes.

But a 'jobs-for-the-boys' mentality also developed, alongside a growing bureaucraticisation of the mining industry. The National Coal Board embarked on major recruiting campaigns, telling young minerstheir future would be secure. And days of prosperity brought a weakening of the old solidarity, the old community spirit. Instead of watching Cowdenbeath Football Club, the more prosperous miners, with the whole of Saturday free, headed out in buses towards the glamorous Ibrox and Parkhead.

What was also happening was that the new methods of coal production did not favour the Cowdenbeath coalfields. Many of the reserves were exhausted, and the existing seams were not suitable for the new techniques. As coàl production from other mechanised pits grew, the demand for coal slumped, largely due to a move towards cheap oil. Towards the end of the 1950s, the National Coal Board shed 70,000 jobs. NCB officials, some of whom were former mine workers themselves, would continually deny that a certain pit was to close, then a few months later it would be unceremoniously shut down. They were looking more and more like the old enemy, the Fife Coal Company. The dream was beginning to fade.

In 1960, the last working pit in Cowdenbeath, the No 7 pit, closed. Its winding gear had overlooked Central Park for many years, so its closure was especially poignant. The town which had grown up on the back on King Coal had no pits left. Local miners had to travel out of the district to work.

Nationally, the mining industry continued to shrink. Miners' leaders argued that in depending on oil from the Middle East and in running down the coal industry, the government was making itself a hostage to fortune. The National Union of Mineworkers still had enough clout in 1974 to take on Edward Heath's govern-ment in the famous 'winter of discontent', reducing the country to sitting by candlelight. But the struggle only masked the fact that the days of glory were nearly at an end. It also made Conservative leaders determined to break the power of a union which could bring the country to its knees.

The fact that this assault could be mounted with popular support in the country indicated a sea change in attitudes to which the big unions themselves contributed. Some of the union barons enjoyed lording it, exercising enormous powers. A few became mirror images of the big capitalist bosses they affected to despise. Power went to their heads as they lost touch with the aspirations of ordinary people. Many of the union leaders had jobs for life – unlike the workers they represented – and they wielded the union block vote with arrogant disregard for democracy. In acting this way, some of the reactionary union barons betrayed their own people. Others, like Arthur Scargill, aligned themselves with East European political leaders, some of whom, in the name of socialism, ran reactionary tyrannies founded on lies and buttressed by secret police. (The churches of the Reformed tradition have a slogan 'Ecclesia semper reformanda' – the church in need of perpetual reformation. The Reformers well understood that unchecked, unaccountable, unredeemed power corrupts and corrupts absolutely, in the church as much as in politics or any other sphere. Cynicism and lies. The doctrine of original sin – mocked by the intellectually slothful as being some kind of melancholy religious pathology – has got nothing to do with literal gardens or snakes or figleaves, and everything to do with the grain of humankind in the raw).

The betrayal of the ideals of ordinary people contributed to the débacle which was to follow, though whether the outcome would have been any different with alternativet actics is a matter for debate. Naïve and foolish ideological posturing could never be a match for well-organised cynical power. The charge of the political Light Brigade into the valley of death could only have one outcome: as in 1921, the enemy had manoeuvred for time and were waiting.

The opportunity came in 1984, and it had all the hallmarks of an ambush. Three years earlier, Joe Gormley had brought the NUM and the government close to confrontation, and Margaret

101

Thatcher had backed off. She was biding her time. In March, 1984, with coal stocks high, Ian MacGregor, chairman of the National Coal Board, made the announcement that he knew would draw the impetuous NUM President, Arthur Scargill, into the fray. Several high-cost pits would reduce production: the timing was calculated, and was determined in conjunction with the prime minister, as his memoirs show.

Scargill, without balloting his members, rushed straight into the trap. He called the miners to battle. "We have two choices," he told the NUM annual conference. "We can give in, as many German people did in the 1930s and allow the worst to happen – we can watch social destruction and repression on a truly horrific scale, and wait for the inevitable holocaust. Or we can fight back. I am not prepared to accept quietly the destruction of the coal-mining industry, nor am I willing to see our social services utterly decimated."

The NUM President announced that British Coal had a further extensive secret 'hit list' of pits which they wished to close: the NCB denied that such plans were in existence. It all sounded so familiar, so ominous. The government's plans were fully pre-pared: and Arthur Scargill, whose ways of working caused friction amongst his own leadership colleagues, and whose demagogic finger-wagging style alienated him from television viewers, became a hated national icon.

The Miners' Welfare Institute in Cowdenbeath once again became a centre for local miners, as the strike dragged on for a whole year. Soup kitchens reappeared. A huge demonstration was held at Central Park, Cowdenbeath, addressed by Mick McGahey.

But it was all over. The miners were defeated. Again. Support in the country was patchy. Many working class people, by now owning their council houses, watching the progress of their shares in the financial markets, reading the Scargill-bashing tabloids and doing quite well, thank you, looked on from the sidelines. A once-proud industry was on its knees, and the once-powerful National Union of Mineworkers was almost bankrupt, amid rumours of financial mismanagement and secret service 'dirty tricks.'

In 1955, over 740,000 miners were employed in Britain; by now, there were fewer than 50,000. The NUM, splintered also by the breakaway Union of Democratic Mineworkers, was compelled to look around to see if there was another union with which they could amalgamate.

The decline of the coal industry had been accelerated by the privatisation of the electricity industry. Suddenly free to choose other sources of fuel, it did just that. Home-produced coal was said to cost £1.51 per gigajoule – the conventional industry yardstick – compared with 90p for imported coal: all this despite a 234 per cent increase in productivity on the part of British Coal during the previous three years.

The miners felt betrayed. They had met all the productivity targets, but they were still heading for the scrap heap. The two problems were the heavy costs involved in British underground mining, and the relative cheapness of the coal imports. A further consequence of privatisation was that distribution companies built their own power stations to weaken the near-monopoly of the generating companies. This led to the so-called 'dash for gas'. The new companies preferred gas to coal power stations, because a coal-fired generator needs more pollution-control equipment and is more expensive to run.

The privatised electricity companies, when asked about redundant miners, simply said that their responsibility was to the consumers and to their shareholders. They had a duty to buy fuel at the cheapest prices, in order to get the best deal for the consumer. The National Union of Mineworkers argued that the government had no national energy policy: to rely on Middle-East oil and cheap coal imports was to make the country a hostage to fortune. The best fuel policy, they argued, must revolve around long-term abundant national resources managed by a skilled workforce: once pits were closed, it would be almost impossible to re-open them – and the skilled workforce would be gone.

The exhausted miners lost the argument. Margaret Thatcher, Cecil Parkinson and the other government ministers preened themselves. Desperate for money to pay off their debts, most miners were compelled to take the redundancy terms on offer, and went on the dole. The devastation to broken mining communities was incalculable.

Pit bings and ruined machinery paid mute testimony to a once-vibrant way of life that would never return. In 1988, the last vestige of mining-related activity in Cowdenbeath disappeared when British Coal (as it was now called) announced the closure of the Central Workshops.

The mining Season in Cowdenbeath was well and truly over.

October, 1992. Michael Heseltine, President of the Board of Trade and Industry, announces in Parliament, almost casually, that 27 pits are to close, and another four are to be mothballed. He says the market for coal is going to be drastically reduced, and regrettably he can see no other option.

He is so sure of his political and economic ground that he has not even involved the Cabinet in the decision. The news is, after all, simply a logical follow-on from the earlier privatisation decisions. He has assumed that the steady pace of pit closures has been accepted by the public as marking the inevitable decline of a once-great industry.

It is the biggest miscalculation of his political career. In the storm which follows in parliament and in the country, the man who would be prime minister is fighting for his political life. The country is shocked by the suddenness and comprehensive savagery of the cuts, and the offhand manner in which the virtual death of the coal industry in Britain has been announced.

Why? What has happened in the last eight years to cause such widespread revulsion? The evangelical zeal for privatisation, so evident in the 1980s, has been tempered as the results have been examined. The privatisation of the electricity industry is now seen as a hasty, botched job, and the 'dash for gas' has been questioned.

Television and newspaper exposure of child labour in the mines of Eastern Europe has made people very uneasy about the cheap imports which have put skilled British miners on the scrap heap, and serious questions have been raised about an energy policy which looks more and more as if it is based on short-term opportunism rather than the long-term interests of the nation. Books about the 1984 miners' strike have shown how much political malice and triumphalism there was on the government's side – and people are now a bit ashamed of the anti-miner hysteria, and even of the role of the police as a semi-political force. Margaret Thatcher has since been replaced by John Major. There is belated shame, too, about the treatment meted out to Arthur Scargill, object of so much national venom. He has been shown to be right in his analysis, even if his tactics were questionable and his demagogery alienating. Yes, there was a secret 'hit list'; yes, the government wanted to teach the miners a lesson which would not be lost on other industrial workers; yes, if the miners lost the battle the industry would be decimated.

Michael Hesltine's achievement is to turn Arthur Scargill into a respectable, reasonable leader. The battered, ageing NUM President is wise enough this time to build on the broad support evidenced in the country, and to appeal to the middle ground. Big demonstrations in support of the miners attract wide-ranging support, with Tory Councillors appearing at rallies denouncing the government policy. Shoppers at Harrods cheer demonstrating miners! Can it be happening?

Mr Heseltine makes a humiliating retreat in Parliament, promising a review of the pit closure policy. The NUM successfully raises the matter in the High Court, winning a verdict declaring that the closure programme is unlawful because the agreed consultation procedures have not been followed.

In Cowdenbeath, there is cynicism. They have seen it all before. They reckon that Heseltine will play for time, and the closures will happen anyway.

They still want to boo the villains, however. But it is confusing.

The leader of the parliamentary opposition to the pit closure programme is Winston Churchill, M.P.

October 3, 1992. Cowdenbeath 1, St Mirren 2.

Has the corner been turned? No. The fans have seen it all before. An Eric Archibald own goal six minutes from time gives St Mirren a victory they hardly deserve.

October 10. Clydebank 4, Cowdenbeath 1.

Peter Lamont is a substitute. He comes on in the second half to great jeers from his former club supporters. Their comments about his girth are not kind.

October 17. Cowdenbeath 1, Stirling Albion 1.

A Willie Callaghan goal in the last minute gives Cowden a point. The fans are pleased that Peter Lamont is on from the start.

On Wednesday, they play Second Division Montrose at Central Park in the B & Q Cup. They should dispose of them, and a good run in the cup will bring them some money.

October 20. Cowdenbeath 0, Montrose 4.

A humiliation. Cowdenbeath have been knocked out of the B & Q cup by a Second Division team. They have been comprehensively cuffed at home by a team featuring their former skipper, Neil Irvine. The pain is made even worse by the fact that their former player Derek Grant has scored two of the goals.

"Harrow must go" is the chant. The correspondence columns of the local paper are full of anger.

October 24. Dumbarton 1, Cowdenbeath 0.

Still losing. Only four of the promotion-winning team are fielded.

October 31. Cowdenbeath 1, Morton 3.

Yet another late goal finishes the match.

It has been a disastrous month: only one point gained, and an early exit from the Cup, 15 goals conceded, and only three scored.

John Brownlie continues to cast his long shadow over the season. Chairman Gordon McDougall defends his decision to withdraw the offer of a new contract for Brownlie, when he testifies at an industrial tribunal in Edinburgh. He denies that he and fellow directors Paul McGlinchey and Ian Fraser had been determined to get rid of Brownlie.

"He asked for incentives despite me telling him again about the severe financial constraints the club were operating under," says the chairman. "If John Brownlie had said on the telephone, 'Okay, I can go with that', John Brownlie would have been re-appointed."

The sad reality is that a fraction of what has been spent on boardroom litigation would have secured Brownlie's future – and the fans know it.

The tribunal is continued until 1993.

November

No one lives by bread and politics alone, but in the pursuit of both men frequently reveal their deepest attitudes and values -- A.J.P. Taylor

As for you, I tell you what the epitaph on you Scottish dissenters will be – pure, but impotent. Yes, you will be pure all right. You will not influence the course of British politics by as much as a hair's breadth. Why don't you get into a nunnery and be done with it? I tell you it is the Labour Party or nothing. I know all its faults, all its dangers. But it is the party that we have taught millions of working people to look to and regard as their own. – Aneurin Bevan to Jennie Lee, 1931.

QUESTION: Which Scottish politician made his debut at Central Park, Cowdenbeath as winner of a 'Bonny Baby' competition?

Answer: Dennis Canavan M.P.

Born in a one-bedroomed council house in Cowdenbeath in 1942, Dennis is proud of that auspicious victory at the home of Cowdenbeath Football Club, even though he is not so sure about the objectivity of the judging process.

"It was a very biased decision, judging from the photograph of the occasion," he tells me with that frankness which characterises all politicians. "The wee girl who was runner-up looked like Shirley Temple, whereas I would have looked like Winston Churchill if you'd stuck a cigar in my mouth. I found out afterwards that the judge was the Provost of Cowdenbeath, a good friend of my grandfather's. Maybe the result was a Labour Group decision!"

Dennis was educated at St Bride's Primary School and St Columba's High School in Cowdenbeath. He played for the school football team alonside the likes of Willie and Tom

Callaghan – Willie went on to play for Dunfermline and Scotland, while Tom played for Dunfermline and Celtic. Dennis left St Columba's as school dux at the age of 15. He later went to Edinburgh University where he graduated B.Sc. with honours in mathematical science. He won a gold medal for the Scottish Universities soccer team which won the British Universities championship, and he played at Central Park for Spartans FC against Cowdenbeath reserves.

Dennis taught for a brief spell at Foulford Primary School, before pursuing a teaching career in secondary education, becoming assistant head of Holyrood High School in Edinburgh. He was elected Labour MP for Falkirk West in 1974, a seat he has held ever since.

Dennis Canavan embodies in his person the different strands of the political, sporting and mining traditions that make up Cowdenbeath. His grandfather's brother, Barney Canavan, played for the Cowdenbeath team which won the East of Scotland Qualifying Cup in 1901; he also received the British Empire Medal for his services to the mining industry – he played a leading part in mine rescue work on many occasions, including the Donibristle and Valleyfield disasters. Dennis's cousin, Denis Jack, played for Cowdenbeath in the 1970s.

It was Dennis' grandfather, Frank Canavan, who was the biggest political influence on his life.

"When I was aged about twelve," Dennis recalls, "he asked me to help him record in writing some personal biographical details about his contribution to local politics and public service. He was born in Carrickmore, Co. Tyrone, Ireland, and his family moved to Cowdenbeath to work in the coal industry in 1884. He left school at the age of ten and went to work down No 7 pit at the age of twelve. He later left the mining industry for health reasons, and was janitor of Foulford School. He was elected to Cowdenbeath Town Council in 1919 and gave a lifetime of public service, particularly through the Labour and trade union movement. Shortly before he died, he received the Freedom of Cowdenbeath, and my mum still has the Freedom scroll hanging on the wall in her home in Perth Road."

Dennis Canavan is a fiery and independent politician who has sometimes been a thorn in the flesh of Labour leaders as well as of the Conservatives. No one doubts the passion of his convictions, which are rooted in the stories of his youth.

"My working class roots in Cowdenbeath undoubtedly helped to forge my socialist convictions, and I frequently return to Cowdenbeath to see relatives and friends and to recharge my batteries. I shall never forget the visits I made to Cowdenbeath Miners' Welfare Institute during the last miners' strike when the local miners and their families put up a heroic struggle to save their industry."

What is his happiest recent memory of Cowdenbeath Football Club?

"Being at Recreation Park, Alloa last year, with my brother Raymond, when Cowdenbeath won promotion to the First Division. It was the most exciting 0-0 draw I have ever seen in my life!"

It was in the miners' long struggle from serfdom to reasonable conditions that the radical political tradition of West Fife was forged. The journey from being chained to the hutches to a humane existence was an arduous and painful and costly one, with more than a few corpses strewn along the black, dusty road.

When I was a teenage reporter on the *Cowdenbeath Advertiser and Kelty News* in the late 1950s, Cowdenbeath Town Council consisted of twelve members. Nine were Labour. The other three were Communist. The Cowdenbeath area also provided the Socialist and Communist leadership of the National Union of Mineworkers. I can well remember a General Election contest in West Fife in which the second most right-wing candidate on the ballot was the fiery anti-Royalist Labour MP, Willie Hamilton! (The other candidates included Lawrence Daly, Independent Labour Party, who left the Communist Party over the Russian invasion of Hungary and became general secretary of the NUM, and James Lauchlan, the Communist Party candidate. The seat had been held for several years by the Communist MP Willie Gallacher). Just as in Victorian Scotland the main choice before people seemed from some accounts to revolve around which branch of Presbyterianism to identify with, in West Fife it was which form of socialism should be favoured.

Although the Communists were committed to ideological Marxism, the mainstream socialism of West Fife grew out of the communalism and co-operation of the pit villages. People were dependent on one another for their livelihood and safety in the face of exploitation and danger; they had to hang together or they would hang separately.

Radical and utopian movements grew up in the wake of the miners' strikes at the end of last century. The Socialist Labour Party won recruits, and *Forward* magazine, edited by Tom Johnston who would become one of the great Secretaries of State for Scotland, sold many copies among miners (its masthead slogan was, "Workers of the world unite; you have nothing to lose but your brains and some of you never had any").

A small and rather eccentric group called the Blatchfordian Socialists would only work four days a week in the pit. One of their leaders, nicknamed 'The Prophet', only worked three days. As Bob Selkirk, a Cowdenbeath political activist observed, most of the miners at this time dreaded dismissal, but it was told of the Prophet that when an exasperated gaffer shouted to him, 'Put on your coat', he calmly and slowly asked, 'An' whit will I dae wi' ma waistcoat?'

Local legend has it that the Prophet was poaching one evening when the laird came across him and shouted, "Don't you know this is my land?"

The Prophet enquired, "An' where did ye get it?"

The laird somewhat haughtily replied, "My ancestors fought for it."

"Aweel," the Prophet said slowly, "we're baith aboot the same size, if ye like I'll fight you for it."

Bob Selkirk comments: "In the days when mining villages had no bus service, no wireless, no film shows, the unorthodox views of the Prophet and his like did mould public opinion in no small measure. The younger miners rebelled against going, as the old miners did, to the pithead a couple of hours or so before starting time. The traditional pictures of Gladstone and Spurgeon came off the walls of the miners' houses."

After the Russian Revolution in 1917, the political debates

became more ideological and more intense. The Labour Town Council of Cowdenbeath were persuaded by fly the Red Flag from the Town House each year on the anniversary of the Russian Revolution. Men who had returned from the war with a hunger for a more just society crowded into halls and on to the streets to hear speakers such as James Maxton, Joe Westwood and Davy Kirkwood.

Home-grown political talent such as Abe and Alex Moffat rose to prominence in the miners' unions. From the vantage point of today's charm-school and television chat show politics, with its bland press releases and insistence on parroting the party line, it is hard to appreciate the robustness and passion of political debate in these early days. The orators honed their skills on platforms and street corners, in pubs and at Temperance Society meetings. The debates were about bread and politics and the direction of society: these were serious men – and women.

One young Cowdenbeath orator who came to national attention was Jennie Lee whose grandfather, Mick Lee, was a well known Fife miners' agent and a leader of some of the early miners' strikes. Jennie was dux of Beath High School, Cowdenbeath in 1922. She had been reared on Socialist Sunday School hymns with words such as:

Through ages of oppression, we bore the heavy load,
While others reaped the harvest from seeds the people
    sowed;
Down in the earth we burrowed, or fed the furnace heats,
We felled the mighty forests, we built the mighty fleets.
But after bitter ages of hunger and despair
The slave has snapped his fetters and bids his foes beware.

She commented in her autobiography, *This Great Journey,* "That sort of thing is not meant to be read in cold blood by grown-up people. They can see all its inadequacies. But our blood was warm, we were young, infinitely impressionable.

"I was completely captivated by the socialist movement and well on the way to becoming a youthful socialist edition of Colonel blimp. I had my prejudices. I had no doubts. I had not the slightest inkling of what went on under the skin of people who did not see things exactly as I did. Idealism, ancestor worship, and a happy feeling that we were the people who would one day revolutionise the world so that 'none shall slave and none shall slay' seemed to me to be just about everything in philosophy, religion and economics that anyone need bother about."

Brought up in an Independent Labour Party household, Jennie was impressed by the big names who came to stay in their home in High Street, Cowdenbeath. One day Clifford Allen, a leading figure in the ILP, came to speak at a meeting in Cowdenbeath.

"By the time the door opened," Jennie recalled, "my eyes were hazy with excitement. I shall never forget the tall, ascetic face and figure of Clifford Allen framed in our kitchen doorway with half a dozen squat dark-looking miners grouped around him. I should not have been surprised if he had suddenly sprouted wings and a halo.

"Later in the evening, when everyone else had gone, he won our hearts all over again by telling us how in prison he and another conscientious objector played an intricate game of chess, one move being made each day by signing to one another when, as prisoners, they were assembled and marched round and round the exercise yard. It was all very elevating. Ours was a wonderful movement. All knights in shining armour who would never rest until the words in the songs of our socialist hymn books had indeed come to pass."

The debates between Communist and mainstream Socialist groups were passionate, and sometimes bitter. Bob Selkirk organised the local Communist Party branch, and he came back from a visit to Russia aglow with evangelical fervour. Young Pioneer groups were organised: hunger marches were held. Selkirk himself, who was banned from working in the Fife coalfields, went to prison several times. The Burgh Police Court was often the scene of political drama. Bob Selkirk recalls one occasion when he was in the dock:

"The presiding magistrate, when opening the case against me said, all in one breath, 'Are you guilty or not guilty, Selkirk, it is all the same what you say, I know you are guilty.' This was too much for Mick Conway, sitting in the body of the court, and he shouted, 'that's not British justice.' He was brought to the bar, and the bailie sentenced him on the spot to ten days in jail."

Bob Selkirk became a member of Cowdenbeath Town Council, at a time when Willie Gallacher was elected Communist MP for West Fife. The Communist attacks on the Labour Party were often vitriolic. Jennie Lee remembered one Communist Party rally.

"After three hours of Communist oratory I crept home feeling dirty and dejected. Whatever I was looking for, this was certainly not it. I hated the nauseating reiteration of the words traitors, fakirs, applied indiscriminately to all and sundry: I was impatient with the cheap quackery of infallibility that all Communist Party spokesmen laid claim to. I found nothing warming, sustaining in this diet of hate and mechanical Marxist clichés.

"This was at best a barren caricature of what I believed a revolutionary socialist party should be. I turned back with a feeling of going home to the broad Labour movement. There, quite plainly, was where I belonged. There were fewer people claiming infallibility in its ranks, there was room for a vigorous exchange of views, there was the hope of turning this vast power-ful organisation that three generations of my family had loved and laboured for, away from the damning influences of MacDonaldism and forward to socialism."

Jennie Lee became a sought-after speaker at political gather-ings, and at the age of 29 the Cowdenbeath firebrand was elected ILP Member of Parliament for Lanark. In Parliament she met the young rising Welsh star of the Labour Party, Aneurin Bevan, and they married in 1935. Bevan, a passionate and charismatic orator, was Minister of Health in the Labour Government which inaugu-rated the National Health Service in 1951. Jennie Lee herself, though often in the shadow of her able, tempestuous husband, eventually became a cabinet minister herself, serving as Minister for the Arts in Harold Wilson's government, and latterly took her place in the House of Lords as Baroness Lee of Ashridge until her death in 1988.

Bob Selkirk supported the Communist Party and the Russian system right to the end. When he retired as a Councillor in 1967 after 32 years service – the year before he was given the Freedom of Cowdenbeath – he wrote in his memoirs *The Life of a Worker:*

"Russia, a backward country under capitalism, is after a short
period of fifty years, leading the world in many spheres, in the
fight for total disarmament, for the liberation of the colonial
peoples, liberation from the cruel and ruthless exploitation by
imperialist monopolies...The Socialist World, pulsating with
youthful vigour, is marching forward confidently, planning and
rebuilding on a tremendous scale, evolving a higher form of
democracy, sparing no effort to win support for the policy of
'peaceful co-existence of countries with differing economic
systems' – the only policy which can save humanity from nuclear
disaster."

In the light of later events in Russia and Eastern Europe, the
touching naïvety of these words of a committed and decent man
are beyond sadness.

The communalist nature of mainstream politics in
Cowdenbeath is best illustrated by the rise of the Co-operative
movement. The Co-op was based not on Marxist doctrine, but on
simple community ideals. Ordinary members of the public became
shareholders in 'The Store,' as it was always referred to in
Cowdenbeath. Each person had a 'Store Number', and each
quarter, a dividend was paid out. The day the 'Divvy' was paid
was always an exciting day, with people queuing up to receive
their dues and rush off to spend them.

The Co-operative movement in Cowdenbeath began in 1871
under the auspices of the Dunfermline Co-operative Society, and
four years later, it became the Cowdenbeath Co-operative Society.
From a membership of 75 that year, it grew to become the largest
trading organisation in the area. The Store expanded into much
larger premises, and hit a crisis in 1896 when a secretary embez-
zled its funds. Despite the fact that no dividend could be paid for
some time, members stayed loyal. The Store emphasised its
sharing quasi-political philosophy at every opportunity. Its annual
gala, 'The Store Treat', was an event which engaged the whole
town, with brass and pipe bands leading the parade past the main
Co-operative shops in the High Street and on to Cowdenbeath
Public Park.

The Store and the 'Toon Hoose' were the twin centres of

power in Cowdenbeath. When I was a boy, the Labour Party and the Co-operative Society ran the town. The Co-operative movement even had its own political candidates, affiliated to the Labour Party.

The prevailing political philosophy was a benevolent municipal socialism, contested by the Communist Party, but supported strongly by the miners' unions and the Store. Housing was the main issue confronting the Town Council. The miners' rows were demolished, and large numbers of council houses built. Inside toilets! Own back and front door! A little garden back and front! The houses may have been painted all the same way, but they represented paradise for many people used to living in squalid circumstances.

One of the pioneers was William Ewing, a miner for 51 years in the No 7 pit, a Labour Councillor for 38 years, and a Provost of the town. His son, Harry, inherited his father's passion for social justice, and is another prime example of the links between mining culture, trade unionism, Labour politics and football which has so characterised the town.

Harry Ewing was born in 1931 in a miners' row in the Kirkford district of Cowdenbeath.

"There were nine of us living in a room and kitchen," he recalls, "and to this day I often wonder how my mother managed to cope. We were not alone. Our experience was repeated time and again, not only in the miners' rows in Kirkford, but throughout Cowdenbeath and beyond. During my political career I have thought often of my early years in Kirkford, and I have come to the conclusion that while we had to get rid of such housing conditions, when we demolished the houses we demolished also a wonderful spirit.

"Families suffered together when someone was ill, and illness was quite common with all the dread childhood diseases."

Harry remembers how his father, through his work in the miners' union, collected money from each family to give to the doctor to ensure that in times of illness they would have medical attention. He went to Foulford Primary School and Beath High School. He cut his political teeth at the age of nine by helping his father and other Labour candidates fight local elections. The

115

enemy was the Communist party.

"I remember in 1938 when we moved from the house where nine slept in two rooms to a new council house where we had nine sleeping in three rooms, the Communist Party painted every street corner in Cowdenbeath condemning my father for corruption.

"I am very proud of the part played in the history of Cowdenbeath by my father, and it was a great honour for the whole family when he became provost in 1952. Cowdenbeath Town Council of that whole postwar period was a council of political giants in my view. It was a council that showed tremendous courage in the rebuilding of the town."

Harry did not follow his two brothers down the pit, but started work as an apprentice grocer with the Co-operative. He ended up working for the Post Office, rising through the union ranks. He could have pursued a career as a full-time union official, but he elected instead to fight for his political aims by means of Parliament. He was elected Labour MP for Stirling and Falkirk in 1971. He served as Parliamentary Under-Secretary of State in the Scottish Office from 1974-79, having responsibility for devolution. He won many plaudits for his gutsy and skilful performances in Parliament.

In 1990, with Home Rule firmly back on the agenda, Harry was asked to be joint chairman of the Scottish Constitutional Convention. The appointment was a tribute to the cross-party regard in which he was held in Scottish political life. He announced that he would retire from Parliament at the next election, and he was given a life peerage. The title he chose, Lord Ewing of Kirkford, reflects his strong family and political roots.

"Influenced as I have been by every aspect of life in Cowdenbeath and Kirkford in work, sport, schools, the church, and by my father and mother, my brothers and sisters, I could not possibly have chosen any other title than that which I now carry with deep humility and great pride."

The 1992 General Election turned out to be a disaster for Labour. Home Rule was a dead duck again.

"If I was starting all over again," he tells me, "I would concentrate on Europe."

Dennis Canavan, M.P., top, and Harry Ewing (Lord Ewing of Kirkford)

With a less arduous life, Harry can now concentrate on one of his first loves – watching the Cowdenbeath football team. As a lifelong Cowdenbeath supporter, he has seen many fine players at Central Park. His favourites?

"Some of the players who came to Central Park stood out and their names remain with me. Jock Shaw, the goalkeeper obtained from Rangers. In the days of the old fashioned shoulder charge no forward in his right mind would go near the burly Jock. Jimmy Hamilton, a right back obtained from Motherwell, 'Breezy Jimmy' as he became known, had first-time tackling down to a fine art and must have been an awesome sight to many an outside left.

"Alex Elliot, a left back who came from the junior ranks, was the most cultured full back I have ever seen playing for Cowdenbeath and a great many other teams as well. Alex actually played his trial against East Fife in a local derby at Central Park. He was in direct opposition to the great and likeable Tommy Adams and Alex played him completely out of the game, so much so that Tommy, out of character, lost his temper and was sent off for giving Alex a kick up the backside.

"On the Saturday following my election to Parliament, East Fife were playing Celtic at Bayview and East Fife very kindly invited me as their guest. Jock Stein was by this time manager of Celtic, and as he was walking to the dugout he spotted Tommy Adams who was by this time retired. Taking Tommy round the shoulders, Jock said: 'That's the first time I've been able to touch you, Tommy, without the referee giving a penalty!' "

Among the other favourites, Alex Menzies was a stand-out for his commitment and inspiration, and another star was winger Johnnie Gilhooley.

"Very slim, slightly built, and prematurely balding, Gilhooley was an absolutely brilliant player. He could do almost anything with a football, and his bodyswerve had to be seen to be believed. I can recall a game against St Johnstone at Muirton Park. Johnnie went for a ball that was dead, and three St Johnstone players were following in close pursuit ready to tackle. When Johnnie got to the ball he swerved, ran past the ball for a good fifteen to twenty yards, and all three St Johnstone players kept following him while the ball remained where it was! He was a joy to watch, and there has been no one with his skill since."

What has it felt like being a Cowdenbeath supporter all these years?

"As a fervent supporter, I've shared with all the supporters the ups and downs, promotion and relegation, the joy and despair, and like every supporter I believed I could make a better job of running the club than whoever happened to be running it at any given time. It was only when I became a Member of Parliament that I came to appreciate that such a feeling was quite common. I can remember when John Prentice was on the verge of being sacked as manager of Falkirk. He turned to me on the Saturday before he was sacked and asked why I was the only person at Brockville who apparently had no criticism of him, to which I answered, 'Well, John, I know what you are going through. I have seventy thousand constituents who are all better MPs than me and you have ten thousand supporters who are all better managers than you. Directors and managers of football clubs are plagued with people who think they can do the job better.'"

Despite the hazards, Harry was thrilled to be invited on to the board of directors of Cowdenbeath Football Club.

"Becoming a director of my home football club was something special to me, and I looked forward with keen anticipation to working with the other directors to build the club into a formidable force. Directors of Second Division football clubs in Scotland must be among the most optimistic people in the world and I was no exception. By the time I became a director of Cowdenbeath I had been twelve years in the House of Commons, five of them as the Under-Secretary of State for Scotland, through the defeat of the Labour Government in 1979, and against that background I really should have known better and been more realistic about the possibilities."

Harry came on to the board not long after the sale of Craig Levein to Hearts, and the club was in a sound financial position. Three years later, a disastrous fire in the grandstand changed all that. It took £80,000 to reinstate the stand, but the insurance money only came to £13,000. Harry had to pick up the cheque at the insurance offices in London, the club were so desperate for the money. One crisis led to another. There was a legal dispute over building works at the ground, and the financial state of the club got steadily worse. Cowdenbeath's plight was known among other clubs, and they had to sell players cheaply simply to keep the overdraft within manageable proportions. Star striker Roddy Grant was sold to St Johnstone for a mere £10,000, and Paul Cherry went to the same club for £14,000.

Some aspects of the work of a director depressed the MP.

"There were players who worked rackets over expenses and complimentary tickets, and it was very saddening," he said. "Some of the players seem to think directors should simply put their hands into their pockets and produce money. I was also saddened by the attitude of the Scottish football authorities, who harangued us about little things. All our people – directors and staff – were part-timers. It was their hobby, and they were giving a lot to the game. The attitude of the SFA and the League left a lot to be desired."

Mr Ewing left the board in 1990 before Gordon McDougall took over, but he supports what the new regime is doing.

"A football club like Cowdenbeath can't be run from miles away," he said. "It's a hobby, and the people involved must be close to it. I left because of the huge debts the club was carrying – I simply couldn't see a way out. Directors have to be guarantors for a lot of money and they risk a great deal – their homes and everything.

"A quarter of a million pounds worth of debt was a millstone round our necks. Clubs like Cowdenbeath can't afford to be in debt like that – they need to operate within their income level. Gordon McDougall has brought a financial discipline to the club which has been lacking since the days of Charlie Gronbach and Davie Fowlis, who didn't allow the club to get into debt.

"I also think it's essential to develop our own young players. Some of the free transfer men we got had learned bad habits and were into all the rackets I've talked about. Some of them didn't have any interest in the club and were trying to get what they could."

Where does he stand on the Brownlie sacking?

"To be honest, if I had still been on the board I would have

120

supported the decision. John Brownlie didn't have a specially good way of dealing with people. He also seemed to be building up a bit of a dynasty, and my view is that things needed clearing out. The timing was bad, just after winning promotion, but the timing for that kind of thing is never good.

"The supporters often accuse directors of not really wanting promotion. I've never met a director, manager or player of any Second Division club who didn't want to get out of the Second Division into the First. I believe McDougall is on the right lines, and the club will emerge again with good young players."

Football has thus far survived the loss of the black diamonds, but what of politics and the Store? Two severe shocks undermined the political certainties of Cowdenbeath.

In the late 1950s, some residents approached the Town Council to request permission to build a garage next to their council house. The request was refused peremptorily. Only Tories had cars, and there could be no concessions. This would be the thin edge of the wedge.

The residents concerned formed themselves into a Ratepayers' Association and put up four candidates at the next municipal election. A third of the Council retired each year: the Ratepayers' Association candidates – whom the Labour Party had dismissed as Tories – swept the board. The following year, the same result. The Ratepayers' Association controlled the Council – what heresy! – claiming the scalps of some of the town's best-known political leaders.

What had happened was that the Labour Party officials had not noticed that the world had changed round about them. The residents with cars were not Tories at all. Quite a number of them were working miners who were making good wages. The miners could not see why they should not be allowed to build a garage next to their home: it hardly seemed to be an outrageous aspiration.

The Labour administration was perceived as arrogant and out of touch, taking people for granted and dispensing patronage too easily. There was a lot of glee in some quarters about their downfall.

There were many tears among the veteran Labour leaders who were voted out of office. They felt they had sacrificed themselves to rebuild the town and build a caring community based on shared values: now they had been unceremoniously booted out by people who could not see further than a car in a garage. The pain was made worse by the fact that some of their opponents were miners enjoying the fruits of better working conditions which the older men had fought for. The older Labour political leaders felt betrayed by their own class.

It was a more chastened Labour leadership which eventually regained power in the Council and kept it until May 1975 when, under local government changes and in a welter of Regional and District newspeak, Cowdenbeath Town Council simply ceased to exist. The Town House was declared a listed building by the Secretary of State for Scotland.

The second shock to the system came twenty years on when the Co-operative Society began to struggle. With no working mines left in the community, the Store's economic base had been slowly eroded. And in the competitive world of supermarkets and multiple trading choice, the Co-operative Society was seen to be old-fashioned and out of touch with modern trends.

The foundations had been well and truly shaken. And the 1992 General Election result was Labour's fourth defeat in a row.

The nights were fair drawing in.

November, 1992. The streets of Cowdenbeath again echo to the sounds of pit boots. As part of the national campaign against the government's pit closure proposal, an eight-man group of Scottish miners, led by the Scottish NUM president, George Bolton, march through Fife on their 400-mile trek on foot to London. At Cowdenbeath, the marchers are guests of honour at a reception given by Provost Margaret Millar and local Councillors. The Provost tells the marchers: "As you know, this district has a good and proud tradition of being a mining community – the villages of West Fife were built around the pits. Unfortunately, we have lost nearly all the jobs in mining, and we understand very well the cause you are fighting and very much support it." But is it a lost cause?

November 7, 1992: Cowdenbeath 0 Hamilton Accies 3

Is the football season a lost cause? The game is effectively over by half time, when former Cowdenbeath striker Kenny Ward put Hamilton two goals up.

The Cowdenbeath fans barrack the team, particularly striker Tom Condie. The fans want Sumo.

Richard McKinlay, a Cowdenbeath supporter from Ayr, writes in the local paper: "Living in Ayrshire, I travel a round trip of 100 miles to watch home games. My enthusiasm for the club, like hundreds, no perhaps thousands of others, was at an all-time high in May. Sadly, mine is in decline and that of others seems to have disappeared completely, looking at recent home gates.

"The board, in their infinite wisdom, chose a novice for manager instead of going for a man with experience, and the performances and results of Cowdenbeath reflect this inexperience. It seems as if already they have resigned themselves to relegation. I ask myself, is there not yet time for a rethink with 28 games left?"

Andy Harrow announces that he plans to have a meeting with the fans to explain his policies. He says: "I hope it will be a constructive meeting and I can help the fans understand why certain decisions they may not agree with have been taken."

The manager puts goalkeeper Steve O'Hanlon up for sale.

The only bright spot is that the Cowdenbeath youth team beat Morton 3-0 in the BP youth cup.

November 14: Meadowbank Thistle 2, Cowdenbeath 0.

Andy Harrow says: "We simply blew it. I feel that we have a few players who are simply not professional enough. They refuse to work hard enough at their skills in training and it shows in matches."

The fans continue to protest. One supporter writes: "A season which promised so much has turned out to be a truly harrowing experience. What has been achieved over the past four years has been systematically destroyed in the short space of four months, and now Cowden find themselves staring relegation in the face after only one season back in the First Division.

"Surely no board of directors is so blinkered by blind faith that they are willing to allow the present state of affairs to continue.

With 27 games to go there is still time to repair the damage and halt our slide back to the basement league.

"Andy Harrow has obviously run out of options after Saturday's defeat by Meadowbank. However, Mr McDougall still has the ultimate option available, and I would hope he will exercise it sooner rather than later. Believe me, it would be the best Christmas present he could give any Cowdenbeath supporter!"

November 21: Raith Rovers 3, Cowdenbeath 0.

The beleaguered manager meets with the angry supporters. He is asked about his own position, and he admits his inexperience as a manager. He points out, however, that he has 20 years experience in football, and that he has no intention of running out on the club, even if the going gets tougher. He pins his faith on the club's youth policy, but is reluctant to subject more young players to the pressures of the First Division for fear of destroying their confidence.

He pleads with the fans to stand by the team, and encourage the players.

The Cowdenbeath youth team beat Whitehill Welfare 1-0 to win through to the quarter finals of the BP Youth Cup.

Dennis Canavan (first baby on the left) winning the bonnie baby competition at Central Park in 1943.

December

I was brought up a Catholic, so I have A-Level Guilt.
– Billy Connolly.

I am plagued with doubts. What if everything is an illusion and nothing exists? In that case, I definitely overpaid for the carpet. If only God would give me some clear sign: like making a large deposit in my name in a Swiss bank. – Woody Allen.

AM I just imagining it when I remember that religion seemed to be a natural thing in the community?

Yes: but it was certainly part of the story by which the community defined its existence.

The first Kirk of Beath was built in the thirteenth century. At the time of the Reformation it hosted a meeting of prominent Scottish Reformers. One of the notable Reformers of the district, the Rev James Durie, was imprisoned for making an attack on the Royal family, and was banished from the city of Edinburgh. The people demanded his return, and he made a triumphal re-entry to the city, living there on a pension of 'sixty six pundes thirteen shillings and fourpence' from the parish of Beath.

It must not be imagined that the place was awash with pious devotion. One contemporary report indicates that instead of meeting on Sunday to hear the minister, young and old assembled and made the 'Lorde's Daye' one of profane mirth. At these meetings a 'pyper' sometimes appeared, and so strong a hold had 'Sautin' that many danced and even played football. Sometimes the men 'fell out and wounded one another'. Beath kirk fell on hard times, and the original pre-Reformation building became a shelter for sheep.

A saviour for the Kirk of Beath came came from, of all places, Kelty. Mr Alexander Colville of that righteous village became tired of the debauchery, and when he was 'stirred by the Lord', he called a meeting at Kelty to promote the rebuilding. The people of the parish were very poor, but so many farmers gave the use of their horses and carts free for the transporting of stones that the new kirk was soon completed. Immediately there was a great revival, with people coming 'out of every citie', so much so that there was hardly any room for the 'pastoure'.

The kirkyard of Beath became a happy digging ground for the agents of Messrs Burke and Hare, until armed farmers kept a nightly vigil. For many years what were presumed to be two iron coffins without lids lay beside the old hearse house. They were, in fact, "safes" placed over new coffins to thwart the bodysnatchers. A large flat stone is still to be found there: it used to be moved into position over a freshly dug grave and could only be removed with the aid of a hoist.

With the rapid expansion of Cowdenbeath as a coalmining centre, and with the influx of people of different backgrounds, there was a need for more – and different – churches. The Auld Kirk (Church of Scotland) , Roman Catholic, Free Church, United Free, Baptist, Brethren, Salvation Army: they were all represented. The story is told of one Church of Scotland member who left the Auld Kirk in Cowdenbeath to join the Brethren. A few months later, he returned to the Church of Scotland. When asked by the minister why he had come back, he replied: "After a while I got tired of religion and decided to come back to the Auld Kirk!"

In common with the gold rush, the coal rush was accompanied by a rash of public houses. The drink trade brought evening solace for men who worked hard all day underground and lived in overcrowded hovels, but it brought hardship as well. A flourishing temperance movement – with several Lodges such as the Good Templars, the Rechabites and the Sons of Temperance – did much to relieve poverty and distress. The weekly meetings of the lodges provided a forum for enthusiastic debaters, and many would-be politicans got their first taste of public speaking at the temperance lodge meetings.

****

How did it all begin, this crazy business of being a minister? There is certainly not a single drop of ecclesiastical blood in my family – they were miners, painters and decorators, mechanics. No religious freaks, thank you.

Did it begin in Eternity, with Yahweh choosing me from the beginning of time? ("One day, saith the Lord, out of Cowdenbeath.....") Or did it begin in the womb?

If it began immediately after the womb, it had all the marks of a dismal failure. The doctor declared me to be the ugliest baby he had ever seen. (If you're going to be ugly, you might as well be the ugliest). A few days later, he told my mother: "Know what I'd do with him?" (point, point). He pulled his hand down on an imaginary toilet chain. He was joking, of course. Wasn't he?

I was a Sickly Child. Soon I had Double Pneumonia, which presumably was twice as deadly as single pneumonia. I was Not Expected to Survive (point, point). A mirror was held to my lips, to check that I was still breathing. What drama! I was hastily baptised at home, with water from the family sugar bowl. How Sweet the Sound. The treatment in those days was to stick on hot poultices and pray. The crisis came. I emerged breathing. Ugly, but breathing. Cowdenbeath Supporters' Club was spared another grievous loss.

Was that the beginning of Grace? (Well, was it? If there's anything I can't stand, sonny boy, it's those preachers who Won't Give a Straight Answer. We Want to Know Where you Stand!)

Well, was it?

The immediate agenda, after the Great Escape, was Survival. Hitler's bombers were blitzing the coalfields and the shipyards. Or was it me, the Lord's Sickly and Ugly Anointed, that the Führer was after? ("Get that Ugly Child from Cowdenbeath," he snarled to Hess). We crouched in the cellar, recognising the drone of the German engines. We would be all right, wouldn't we?

The family across the road were not all right. A German plane plunged into their house, killing all the occupants. My father, hearing that a plane had crashed among the council houses at the top of Stenhouse Street, rushed home, relieved to find us safe.

Luck, says Aristotle, is when the other guy gets hit with the arrow.

And God? Where was He in all this?

If there's anything I can't stand, it's those gods who Won't
Give a Straight Answer

My first ostensibly religious experience occurred at Foulford
primary school when I was eight years old. (Ah, Foulford primary
school! What a collection of stuffed birds you boasted! One boy
stared at them intently, in the big glass cage, and inquired of the
head teacher: "Haw sur! Dae ye ken that a' your burds are deid?")
   One of my classmates, Andrew Cree, had been knocked down
and killed in Cowdenbeath High Street by the Kirkford bus. An
eye-witness in the class said that Andrew's 'puddens' (his insides)
had been lying in the street. We were awestruck by this sudden
visitation of Something, through the agency of that most familiar
of objects, the Kirkford bus. Miss Dawson, our teacher, came in
and told the hushed class that Jesus had Taken Andrew Up to
Heaven. We then stood and sang the familiar hymn

When He cometh, when He cometh
To make up His jewels,
All His jewels, precious jewels,
His loved and his own.
Like the stars of the morning,
His bright crown adorning,
They shall shine in their beauty,
Bright gems for His crown.

Little children, little children
Who love their Redeemder,
Are the jewels, precious jewels,
His loved and His own.
Like the stars of the morning.....

The voices are still in my head. We sang it with tears and wonder
and fear and sadness. We emphasised the words. Jew-ells, we sang
each time. Despite the talk about jew-ells and bright crowns and stars
of the morning, we knew that the world was a frightening place.
German planes. Even the friendly old Kirkford bus. Agents of death,
filling up the spaces in Kirk of Beath cemetery.
   An accordion-playing evangelist set up his van outside the

Foulford school gates and shouted to us about Jesus, who had Come Down from Heaven to Save us from our Sins. He was the one who had Taken Andrew Up. I remember feeling the pleasant and relieving glow of Yahweh in my belly. A school friend felt likewise. We repaired to a local hill, down which we proceeded to roll, reciting the Lord's Prayer (this being the best way of praying without it being obvious). We dug a hole and left a notebook and pencil as gifts for the Lord. Next day they were gone. We were delighted. Well done, Yahweh! We learned later that a local youth, who bore no resemblance to the Lord whatsoever, had been seen with them.

Since then, I have been sceptical about religious enthusiasm.

Cairns Church, Cowdenbeath was my spiritual home. It was a former United Presbyterian Church, now Church of Scotland. My grandfather was an elder of the kirk. On Saturdays the founding father sat at the front of the stand at Central Park, with a big tartan rug round his knees, and on Sundays he was in the family pew. Every week. Christian values were assumed, without question and without articulation.

A patriarchal figure, a man with a reputation for doing a good job of work as a painter, he expected to be served by the women of the family. Alex Ferguson represented a solid, dependable, tried and trusted way of life in which everybody, especially 'the womenfolk' knew their place and learned to win their rewards through humouring and cunning rather than by outspoken advocacy.

My father was a regular kirkgoer. He declined the invitation to become an elder because he liked the horses as well as a drink at the local bowling club, and felt that gambling and eldership didn't go together. My mother, a librarian, had been compelled to leave school early because there was not enough money in her family to pay for her education, a fact which she resented all her life. She also deeply resented the patriarchy and it was this, more than anything, which kept her from a church which worshipped the God of our Fathers.

I was sent to Sunday School, where the rudiments of the faith were taught me by Kate Simpson, who worked for a local printer. Cairns was what I would now define as a 'broad' Church of

Scotland kirk. It was served in my time by what I recognise as superb parish ministers – Douglas Potter, Bill Nicholson, David Grieve and Angus Macleod. They were all men of evangelical concern in the broadest sense: loving pastors and preachers who brought good news without believing it was a sin to think.

When I remember the church of my youth, I think warmly of it, probably idealistically. The singing! I can still hear it: the metrical psalms sung to Dunfermline, Kilmarnock, Martyrs, with strength. As, in my mind's eye, I rove around the congregation, I can see plenty of men. Miners with rough hands. At home in worship. Engaging fully and without embarrassment in a natural activity.

When I think of that church of my youth, I grieve for something which was robust and simple and strong, and is gone forever.

Ah, but sin is never far away, as the preachers were fond of pointing out. At fourteen, I took up smoking. A boy stood guard at the school toilets while we puffed away on 'doups' we had found in the gutters. At home, when no one was around, I would steal my mother's Senior Service cigarettes and puff the smoke up the chimney. What valour! what bravado!

More crime. Some of us went into the local Woolworth's store and lifted small, useless things from the counter while someone distracted the lassie. Success went to our heads. We decided to go in for the big time, and organised raids on Dunfermline Woolies! Jings! The city of Dunfermline! And all this without a theory about the redistribution of wealth. If any of Cowdenbeath's finest are reading this, I will come quietly. This file can now be closed.

Where was Cairns Church in all of this? Fairly distant. I had Decided Not to Go Back.

When the headmaster of Beath High School heard that I wanted to be a journalist, he was furious. Journalism to him ranked well below prostitution in the moral league table. Since I had passed my Highers, he wanted me to go to university and get a decent job, like teaching. But I Knew my Own Mind.

I started as a cub reporter with the *Cowdenbeath Advertiser and Kelty News* at the age of sixteen, earning £2 10s 6d a week. The paper was owned by Alex Westwater, a local historian and philanthrophist. The editor, George Hutchison, was the local correspondent for most of the press in Britain. The rest was handled by Bob Holman, for whom I also worked. The three of us covered everything: the local council, the police courts, pit disasters, greyhound racing. And, of course, the football. I reported on the home games every week, for all the papers, and travelled to the away games in the team bus. Not a cliché left unturned. How marvellously convenient that there were always three best on each side! I was amused when people quoted what the *Sunday Post* said about the game, in contrast to the *News of the World's* view. It was only me all the time.

The 'dugs' were an essential part of mining town culture. Go down any street and there would be a miner walking with his lean whippet. The dog track was a place where a week's pay packet could easily be lost in an evening, especially following my tips. There were various tricks for putting a favourite out of the running, like feeding it a mince pie, or jabbing it in the backside with the point of the then fashionable winkle-picker shoes. There were those who knew about these things (wink, wink).

Since then, I have never believed anything I read in the papers.

Death was never far from the surface of a mining community. Literally.

The Lindsay Pit disaster. I was the reporter for most of the Scottish press. How could I forget the anxious women, pale, strained faces framed by headscarves, waiting at the pithead for news of their menfolk? Or the black-faced, ashen men who worked round the clock in a vain attempt to rescue their colleagues? Or the way in which the community rallied round the bereaved, surrounding them with inarticulate love?

I had to visit the relatives, to get their stories. I found myself being a pastor as well as a newshound. I couldn't help it. But it left me with questions about this strange Yahweh.

I learned that the price of coal has to be measured in a calculus of human blood. Yes, and black stained lungs.

The miners, they said, are asking for too much money.

I remember the quiet dignity of the miners in their best suits, walking silently behind the coffins to Beath kirkyard: their reverence at the graveside as the minister intoned the text "Greater love hath no man than this, than a man lay down his life for his friends", before speaking about David Scott, who had perished as he went back to try to rescue his trapped colleagues: the tears that rolled down the strong faces.

Well, God?

I spent a lot of time talking to Bob Selkirk, enthralled by his stories. His partisan history of the struggles with the Fife Coal Company became part of my history. I relived the lockouts and the soup kitchens and his times in prison. I went to political meetings at which fiery speakers argued that the miners had been exploited by the coal owners who kept the profits and were now living off the compensation they had been paid. I was taught that capitalism was the name of a profound evil which separated brother from brother; that the only solution was for the workers to band together, to overthrow the ruling class and to establish a brotherhood based on equality and justice. It was a wonderful vision, and it came to me like a religious conversion. What communicated to me was the passion of the thing: the hot search for justice. It reminds me of Søren Kierkegaard's phrase: "Purity of heart is to will one thing". Blessed are they that hunger and thirst after righteousness, for they shall be filled.

I learned the meaning of commitment through watching Bob Selkirk sticking at his task, day after day, despite the fact that the evidence daily pointed away from Britain ever becoming a Soviet satellite. Even when I found myself increasingly questioning his certainties, he was, and remains, my paradigm of commitment. He is in my pantheon of heroes, one of the saints who willed one thing, a Communist Councillor who nudged me in the direction of the ministry.

Pity about the gulags, though.

And the Church? Where was the Church in all this?

That was precisely the question raised by the Rev Cameron Mackenzie as he rose to address a mass meeting of miners in the Cowdenbeath picture house. They had come together to protest against the proposed closure of local pits.

These men had been reared in the socialist tradition. But now, bewilderingly, the enemy was not the evil coal owners, but the National Coal Board, the state enterprise which only a year or so previously had launched a big recruiting drive for more miners.

Cameron Mackenzie lifted the men to their feet with his statement that the Church stood firmly behind them in their struggle, and that he would be glad to be part of the miners' deputation to London. His speech sent goosepimples up and down my spine.

Could Christianity match its personal liberation with a passion for social justice?

It was Alex Smith who got me back to church. He was an elder of Cairns Church, and he was the best-read man I have ever known. He took me under his wing, as did Tommy Deas, a local slater and head of the Cowdenbeath fire brigade. They were mentors, fellow nudgers. Welcome to the pantheon.

In Cairns Church Youth Fellowship I learned to come out of my shyness, to flex my muscles: literally. I embarked on a Charles Atlas course to help turn a molehill into a mountain. Farewell Sickly Child! Hello Adolescence! Oh God.

Most week nights we gathered at Demarco's, the local café, slowly sipping hot oranges through evenings of stupefying boredom, scared to go home in case we missed something. There we were, the flower of Cowdenbeath: crew cuts, garish waistcoats, white drainpipe jeans, brown swede shoes. (My aunt pursued me along High Street, spun me round, looked me up and down, and exclaimed, "In the name of the wee man!", before going sadly home).

I played banjo in a jazz band, the Saints All-Star Rhythm Group, which had a meteoric rise to fame and an equally meteoric decline. One week, Scottish Television: next week, two dizzy nights topping the bill at Lochgelly Cinema de Luxe: next week, Gray Park Women's Guild, the West Fife equivalent of Valhalla. In the youth fellowship we intrigued against each other, during and after endlessly tortured business meetings, but united in blaming everything on Them – parents, elders, kirk session. I rose through the ranks to become president. I didn't always blush when

133

I spoke. What progress! I even preached at the youth fellowship service – a 'daring' lecture to the older generation about how unchristian they all were.

Oh God.

The YF was an excellent place for boy-meets-girl, and for the fumbling, squirting, grotesque and sometimes tender experiments which went on whether They liked it or not. Especially because They didn't like it.

And sometimes we explored matters of faith.

Life continued to pose questions that were not easily answered. I got a tip-off about a serious accident on the Cowdenbeath-Kelty road. I got there before the medical services. A person, impossible to tell whether a man or a woman, was lying at the roadside, face a mask of blood, moaning horribly. Out of the wrecked car hung the arm of a dead man.

The silent wheels of the Lindsay pit: the silent shuffling of the men in their shiny suits, following the coffins: the silence at Beath cemetery, broken only by the preacher's text: the silence of an afternoon between Cowdenbeath and Kelty shattered by the blood-soaked screams of a broken, dying human animal: what did that silent darkness mean? And what could I do about the inadequacy I felt in the face of that dark side?

Evenings at Demarco's were not enough. I longed for deliverance from dark questions of red blood and black dust, and from guilt brought about by remembrance of trivial sins raised to the status of cosmic dramas. I yearned for a personal encounter which would resolve everything from acne to world peace.

Enter, unambiguously, a fundamentalist Christian organisation. Their Scottish students held missions in towns where an invitation had been extended by local churches.

And they Knew Where they Stood.

I was spellbound. The testimonies – "I used to have terrible doubt/anxiety/unhappiness until I welcomed Jesus into my heart, since when I have perpetual joy/certainty/peace" – were delivered with excited conviction. 'Christ is the Answer' was the slogan on the banner they strung across Cowdenbeath High Street.

I did not succumb immediately. I started a correspondence with one of the students; eventually I wrote to him, giving him the news he yearned to hear: I had made a Decision for Christ. I told my assiduous counsellor that I had read the works of Bertrand Russell, and it had left me dissatisfied: the truth of the matter was that I had read very little of Russell, but felt somehow that my testimony had to conform to an evangelical stereotype which painted the old life in hyperbolic dark lines, and the contrasting new life in garish colours. Joy! Joy! Uncontrolled Joy!

I must have been a frightful prig, witnessing to the Cowdenbeath damned. The zealous, earnest students had taught me to write off my ordinary church experience. "Being brought up in a Christian home doesn't make you a Christian any more than being brought up in a garage makes you a car" was one of the choice gems I regurgitated when the correct button was pressed.

Oh God. Theological brain death.

I prayed, I read the Bible, I prayed again.

But world peace did not come. Even the plooks remained, despite the wonder-working blood. So did the dark questions. Thank God. I knew in my restlessness that my questions could not be resolved within the constricting framework of fundamentalist ideology. I did not regret the converting experience, but I knew instinctively that I could not continue to seek the living God among the claustrophobic tombs of authoritarian sign-here-or-else be-damned religion. But where could my questions be taken seriously? Back in Cairns Church. David Grieve was a sympathetic pastor, possessed of a living faith and a healthy scepticism about prefabricated answers.

After four years with the *Cowdenbeath Advertiser and Kelty News,* I worked for three years in the big city of Edinburgh. As I assembled with my journalistic colleagues in our usual haunt, Baillie's Bar, after the City Final edition of the *Edinburgh Evening News* had gone to press, I broke the news that I was leaving to go to university. I was going to study for the ministry.

George Millar, that doyen of Edinburgh journalists, had his pint half way to his mouth. His eyes were like organ stops.

"Jesus Christ!" he exclaimed.

My old headmaster was pleased. My father was bewildered. My half-believing, non church-going mother was proud.

So where did all this ministry stuff start? I don't know. All I do know is that whenever I am absolutely sure I Know Where I Stand, I feel a strange choking sensation in my lungs.

Dark, blood-stained coal dust.

******

December 2, 1992. St Mirren 5, Cowdenbeath 0.

The procession of goals is an embarrassment. Billy Lamont is sent off at 0-0. St Mirren goalkeeper Campbell Money scores with a penalty.

December 5. Cowdenbeath 2, Kilmarnock 3.

Cowden play much better, and give promotion-aspiring Kilmarnock a hard game. Eric Archibald is sent off for punching George McCluskey. A pleasing note is the performance of young Dominico Maratea who makes his first team debut at left back.

December 8. Cowdenbeath 2, Ayr United 2.

Cowden twice come from behind. Willie Callaghan and Graham Buckley get the goals.

December 12, 1992: Cowdenbeath 1, Clydebank 3

The attendance of 298 is the lowest for any senior game in Britain that day.

The creaky defence collapses again. Only five of last season's promotion-winning squad are in the side. Willie Syme has gone junior, and is scoring goals for Lochore Welfare.

Cowdenbeath are marooned at the bottom of the table, with only 5 points. Their nearest rivals, Stirling Albion, have 14 points.

A banner is strung up across part of the terracing at Central Park. It says simply "Harrow Must Go".

December 19: Dunfermline Athletic 4, Cowdenbeath 1.

Another hammering from the Auld Enemy. What a humiliation!

Andy Harrow: "I thought we did well enough in the first half. The Pars had been booed off at the break, and if we had kept it at

136

1-1 into the second half they would have started to struggle. Alas, we lost that second goal and we just could not cope as they stepped up the pace late in the game."

December 26: Hamilton Accies 4, Cowdenbeath 0

Another disaster, with Cowdenbeath completely out of their depth. Kenny Ward scores again.

"It was one of our poorest showings of the season,"says the manager."We played as individuals and did not back one another up."

Fans' favourite, midfielder Gus Malone, and goalkeeper Steve O'Hanlon decide to go junior with Dundee St Joseph's. Cowden get £3000 for Malone, who gets a similar sum as a signing-on fee. Why is it that players would rather play junior football than continue in the First Division with Cowdenbeath?

Another favourite of the fans, striker Graham Buckley, is transferred to Second Division Arbroath for £6,000. Chairman Gordon McDougall says: "We were reluctant to let him go, but Arbroath made him a magnificent personal offer and we could not stand in his way."

Effectively this means that Second Division and junior teams are offering better terms than First Division Cowdenbeath.

The chorus of disapproval continues.

"Cowdenbeath FC have treated their fans to one of the most embarrassing seasons in the club's history," writes one supporter in the local paper. "Mr Brownlie's face didn't fit so he was fired, and since then it has been defeat after defeat. The club have shortchanged their loyal support and not for the first time. Cowden would have been better not winning promotion at all if they had no plans to do anything when they got into the First Division.

"It would seem a boycott of matches is the only way to bring change, as currently the club don't deserve the money."

What a miserable end to a miserable year! Cowdenbeath are anchored at the foot of the First Division, with an embarrassing five points to their credit. They have recorded no home wins, and have conceded goals. They have been drawn away to Premier League Partick Thistle in the Scottish Cup, so will make an early exit.

The promotion-winning team has been broken up, and first team players are heading for the exits. Relegation looks a certainty. The fans want the dismissal of the manager and the chairman, and are threatening a boycott.

A Happy New Year.

Professor Sir James Black

January

If God spare my life, ere many years I will cause a boy that driveth a plough shall know more of the Scriptures than thou dost! – John Tynedale to a bishop, 1521.

Football may be an athletic profession, but it is also a borstal for wayward genius – Stuart Cosgrove.

WHAT DO the following have in common?

Professor Sir James Black, Nobel Prize Winner; Tom Gourdie, OBE, artist, teacher and handwriting expert; Fred Stiven, head of design, Gray's School of Art; Professor Duncan Reekie, chairman of the Department of Economics, Johannesburg University; Elspeth King, author and former curator of the People's Palace, Glasgow; John McCracken, Director of Customer Relations, IBM; Derek Ferguson, managing director of S.G. Warburg, Merchant Bankers; Blair Malcolm, managing director, Blyth & Blyth, consultant engineers; Dr James Syme, Vice President of the Royal College of Physicians and Consultant at the Western General Infirmary, Edinburgh; Professor Agnes Jarvie, Chair of Nursing, Glasgow University; Professor Richard Scott, Chair of Medicine, Edinburgh University; Professor Gillies, Chair of Clinical Bacteriology, Queen's University, Belfast; Professor Philip, Chair of Infectious Diseases and Immunology, Bowman Gray School of Medicine North Carolina; John Baxter, vet, television celebrity, and author of *It's a Vet's Life;* Elaine Hall, opera singer, Covent Garden; James Paterson, star of *Phantom of the Opera;* Stuart Adamson, *Big Country* star; Lewis Morrison, principal clarinet player with Scottish Opera; Alan Hutchison of the *Scotsman,* several times winner of the Scottish Journalist of the Year award; Baroness Lee of Ashridge (Jennie Lee), former Minister of the Arts; Baron Ewing of Kirkford, former Under Secretary of State,

Scottish Office; Jim Baxter, celebrated Rangers and Scotland footballer; Jim Leishman, former manager of Dunfermline Football Club; and so on.

The answer is that they were all educated at that international seat of higher learning, Beath High School, Cowdenbeath. And graduates of St Columba's R.C. school in Cowdenbeath include Denis Canavan, MP; Gerry Eadie, owner of C.R. Smith; and Willie and Tom Callaghan of Dunfermline and Scotland and Dunfermline and Celtic respectively.

The first Beath school owed its origins to John Knox. The great Scottish Reformer argued passionately for a school in every parish, a visionary scheme which was adopted in 1616. The session records of Beath Parish show that the first schoolmaster appointed was one Thomas Deas, in the year 1697. The school was administered by the kirk session and a group of landowners, who raised the money for the schoolmaster's salary. Knox's dream was that every boy should have an education, no matter his family background, and many a 'lad o' pairts' from Beath parish went on to university education. The pupils were taught reading, writing, grammar and scripture. They were encouraged to go on to study Latin and Greek. The Reformers wanted a literate Scotland which could read the scriptures in the vernacular.

The Beath parish school is described in *A History of Fife,* written around 1840, as follows: "The school has been for some years admirably taught by the present teacher, Mr Alexander Bethune and his brother who preceded him. The average number of scholars is about 100. The school room and the teacher's dwelling are excellent and commodious. The salary is the maximum."

In 1872, parish schools came under the direction of school boards. By the 1890s, when Cowdenbeath's expansion was in full flood, its population having risen from 1252 to 8296 in forty years – a 700 per cent population increase – free education was available to every child.

Beath High School was built on coal. Literally. The building had to be shored up a few years after it was erected because of underground workings. It stood over the old workings of the

Cowdenbeath No 8 pit, and the active workings of the No 7 colliery. Like several other buildings in the town, the three-storey school with a fine sandstone exterior sank slowly into the ground, but it did not do so uniformly. One end of the building was nearly five feet lower than the other: two class rooms disappeared below ground level, and at the other end of the building some of the windows almost vanished into the ground. Once it was discovered that access to the disused underground classrooms could be gained from a first floor French classroom, daring pupils would disappear during boring classes and reappear covered in grime. Walking through the school was always an interesting and unpredictable experience: Beath High was a finishing school for the Ministry of Silly Walks.

The school made headline news in the 1970s, when a pupil from Cowdenbeath was suspended for refusing to take 'the strap' after a breach of discipline. His parents appealed to the European Court of Justice at the Hague, and won. The case was a landmark in the fight against corporal punishment in schools, and in 1984 the 'belt' was banned from Scottish schools.

It is ironic that Cowdenbeath should be the place at which the power of the strap was finally broken, since the offending instrument of torture – ouch! I can still conjure up the unjust pain of six lashes from a psychopathic metalwork teacher for the terrible crime of tapping a pupil on the shoulder while walking down the sloping, underground basement corridor – was actually made in the town! The leather belts were originally manufactured in Lochgelly, giving the fearsome 'tawse' its nickname. The firm of Dick the Sadlers, manufacturers of the strap, transferred part of their business to Cowdenbeath, and at the time of the celebrated court case, 2000 straps a year (XH 'Extra Heavy' being the most feared version) were being exported from Cowdenbeath to many parts of Scotland.

The mining community held education in high, almost reverential, regard. Education was the panacea for political troubles: once the working classes were educated they would throw off the yoke of the oppressors. Jennie Lee, dux of the school in 1922, was often cited as a role model. She herself felt that too much reverence was given to university degrees.

141

"The universities were turning out ten-a-penny graduates in large droves several times a year. Most of us remained largely illiterate. For some months before examinations, we crammed to the teeth. A month or two afterwards, we had forgotten all we had learned. All that remained were our certificates, and in the case of those who were particularly obtuse, a feeling of superiority over people who had not been initatied into these mystic rites.

"But often at my meetings I saw the faces of elderly and middle-aged colliers looking up towards me from the body of the hall, reconciled to my youth because of the letters after my name. It is part of Scottish working-class pride to deny any respect for university degrees, but part of its practice, particularly inside the Labour movement, to pay far too much deference to them. I knew how my grandfather's, even my father's, generation felt about education. They were very romantic about it. They thought of it as a kind of lamp to light the feet of their children, so that we need not stumble and hurt ourselves as they had done, or as armour buckled around us so that we could meet in fair fight all who stood in our way. They never doubted that our fight would be anything other than their fight and with them and of them and for them."

Education was seen as the way out of the pits. Miners wanted their sons, in particular, not to have to spend their daily lives under the earth. Not for them the romantic view of the coal industry promoted by the drawing-room socialists who would not even be dragged screaming underground: the pit was a prison, and education represented the key to the prison door.

James Whyte Black is a genius. And he comes from Cowdenbeath.

There are those who would regard these two statements as mutually exclusive: but Jim Black is an exceptional example of the educational values of a mining community, and of Beath High School in particular.

Born in 1924, James Black chose not to follow his engineer father into the mines. He showed outstanding ability in science and maths at Beath High School, and at fifteen he won a bursary for St Andrews University. His brilliance marked him out for a distinguished career, and he soon gained lectureships at St Andrews and at Glasgow Veterinary School, where he set up the physiology department. In 1958 he moved to ICI. It was after the death of his father as a result of a heart attack that he turned his attention to coronary problems.

At that time, scientists were searching for ways to increase the oxygen supply to the heart muscle when it was deprived of adequate blood because of narrowing of the arteries. He decided to invert the proposition, and try to decrease the demand. Adrenalin was known to increase the demand for oxygen, and he set about devising a drug with the same biochemical shape as adrenalin. The exciting result was Inderal (anagram of adrenalin), the beta-blocker drug. His discovery prolonged and indeed saved the lives of many sufferers from coronary disease, and Inderal became the biggest-selling drug in the world.

In 1972, by which time he was working for Smith-Kline, Black produced another brilliant 'first'. At his laboratories he produced Tagamet, a revolutionary drug which transformed life for ulcer sufferers. Treatment for ulcers had mainly been surgical; the outstanding success of Tagamet made it the world's best-selling drug, ahead even of Inderal.

James Black became Professor of Pharmacology at University College, London in 1973, and eleven years later was appointed to the chair of Analytic Pharmacology at King's College Hospital, London, where he has a free hand to develop new lines of research, funded by J & J Johnson.

"He can pursue whatever he thinks is worthy," says a spokesman for Johnsons in America. "Who in the world would one more wish to be associated with? Wherever that fertile and inventive mind goes will be beneficial." In 1988, Sir James Black's international track record was recognised when he was awarded the Nobel Prize for Medicine. Professor Desmond Laurence, of University College, London, commented: "Black in the laboratory has relieved more human suffering than thousands of doctors in a lifetime at the bedside." Professor Michael Oliver of the Royal College of Physicians in Edinburgh, described him as "a humble and quite brilliant man always full of exciting and original ideas."

Two years later he was voted "Scot of the Decade" in a *Scots-*

man poll. At the award ceremony, Mr Gus Macdonald, managing director of Scottish Television, described Professor Black as "an example of the thrawn, questing, purposeful intellect traditionally bred in these parts."

A modest, but combative and fearless man, Jim Black has no doubts at all about the roots of his successful career – his home and school at Cowdenbeath. His father worked his way through the coal mines until he became a pit manager, and he encouraged his family to study. The reverence for education can be seen in the fact of his five sons one became a doctor, one became a Church of Scotland minister, one a psychiatrist in Vancouver and one a teacher. The combination of the respect for education and the quality of teaching at Beath High School set James Black on his way.

"Teachers in Scotland then had a vocation," he emphasises. "Beath High School was sitting on an old worked-out mine, and was sinking into the ground like a drunk on crutches. But Dr Waterston, the man who taught maths, was a scholar. He was one of the great teachers of his day – a man with tremendous intellectual confidence."

In 1989 Sir James made a sentimental return to Beath High School, to present prizes. He sat down at his old desk at the science laboratory exclaiming – "It's absolutely as it was!". The visit to Cowdenbeath was marked by an announcement by Smith, Kline and French laboratories that they were setting up a Sir James Black Scholarship trust fund, worth £70,000, to provide up to two scholarships a year for Beath students going to university to study science or medicine.

The most celebrated graduate of Beath High School, though, is not one of its many distinguished academics, but a local and national folk hero with the most educated left foot in Scottish football history – one James Curran Baxter.

'Slim Jim' Baxter is widely acknowledged to be one of the most gloriously gifted footballers the world has seen. Even the great Pele of Brazil (the yellow, rather than the blue variety) remarked that he wished Baxter had been born a Brazilian. The willowy, wispy Jim had the Hooky Leonard ability to stroll around the pitch with the ball apparently tied to his instep – yes, to bring down the ball from waist height and sweep it fifty yards to an unmarked team mate all in one graceful movement. His vision and balletic balance were extraordinary. He also had Hooky Leonard's love of tormenting the panting, pursuing opposition: what made him such a national hero was that as a Scottish internationalist he loved provoking the English. As with Hooky, the opposition fans had a great desire to stone him.

Jim Baxter also had Leonard's self destructive qualities: he hated training, fell out often with his superiors, and drank far to much for his own and others' good.

Jim was born in 1939 in Hill o' Beath, a mining village on the outskirts of Cowdenbeath. Here is how he remembers his early days:

"Home was a miner's row. Everybody in the family was, or had been, down the pit, and when I look back, I think of those days as great times, though I'm not sure why. I mean, there's not really much to enjoy in a pit village, not by the standards of most people anyway. Four in a bed and outside toilets, mince and potatoes the pride of the menu....some way, you might say, from the so-called sophistication I was to sample in later years.

"Somebody once said to me, yes, but it must have been character-forming. What's that supposed to mean? These are the kind of clowns who embarrass miners by calling them the salt of the earth, that sort of thing. They've never been in a pit village – except maybe to pass through in a hurry, thinking, how quaint! They've never had a Co-op number, they always have dinner in the evening, they drink half pints and they think they're daring, but they feel they should identify with what they like to call the working-classes. There is, to be sure, a sense of togetherness, even clannishness, among miners and mining folk, probably because they know that if they don't help each other nobody else will. It could be that a mining village childhood does form character, but if you go down the pit often enough, it also forms black bits on your lungs."

There were a lot of good footballers at Beath High School, and Jim took a while to break into the first team. When he left school at fifteen after failing to make any impression on the academic records, he got work as an apprentice cabinet maker. Six months later the lure of bigger money took him to Fordell Colliery where he worked at the colliery 'tables', separating coal from stone. He played football at the local parks on Sundays, and had some games for Cowdenbeath Royals, the local 'nursery' club. Then he signed for the local junior side Crossgates Primrose, being given a signing on fee of £50.

"I held the money in my hand, and I could hardly believe it," he recalls. "I had never seen so much money in my life. It wasn't a cheque. Hard cash. Used one-pound notes, believe it or not. I felt capable of ransoming somebody, leaving it in a suitcase on a lonely road somewhere. Instead, not knowing anybody who had been kidnapped, I bought my mother a shining new washing machine, and she loved it. I'm sure it must have been about the first of its kind in that part of Fife."

As a skinny, underweight outside left, Jim had to learn to survive in the fierce battleground of Fife junior football. Several referees were chased out of town. (As a young reporter, I used to cover two or three junior games on the same afternoon, travelling between them by motor scooter. Jim Butchart, the Crossgates Primrose secretary, would give me the teams, and add ritually: "Jesus Christ is the referee as usual!" The junior grounds were no places for shrinking Primroses or Violets – so why were so many clubs called by such names?)

Baxter was a standout in the Fife football wars, often mentioned in my despatches to the *Evening News, Evening Times, Sunday Post* and *Sunday Mail*. To survive, he had to be nimble.

"If you're underweight and, well, sort of learning, you are put out on the wing – out of the way of the heavy stuff in the middle of the park, where they don't take prisoners and don't even bother to inform the next of kin.

"So, in my first Scottish junior cup tie, I'm playing outside left, and the opposition is Tranent Juniors. I'm not quite seventeen years old at the time, and I weigh about nine stone, soaking wet. But of course I've got lots of confidence, even if there were some who thought I had too much of that. We're lining up at the start, and I look casually over at the right back.

"It's not that I was a coward, you understand, but there was nothing wrong with my sense of self-preservation. The man was maybe six feet tall, but he looked like a blend of King Kong, Ernest Borgnine and Bobby Shearer. In fact he made Bobby Shearer look like Danny La Rue, and Bobby could handle himself very well. You may say to yourself, ah, but a real player can always make a monkey out of a gorilla. That's a good theory. It pre-supposes that you get tackled only when you've you've got the ball. I've played in dozens and dozens of matches where that theory is nothing better than a poor joke. I've been kicked up in the air when nowhere near the ball, and so have plenty of other folk. It's called teaching a lesson, and I was beginning to learn that lesson as early as sixteen.

"I don't pretend to remember exactly what happened during that game, but I do remember having what the scribes would call a quiet match. If I did get the ball in space, I got shot of it right away, and then jumped as high as I could. That's another lesson that has to be learned early. If you don't jump high enough, you're in trouble. Even so, you can jump six feet from a standing start, and there are still lads who'll get you on the way down. Usually, they're not sent off, and they're really laughing."

The heavies could not tame the precocious skills of the skinny one who, like Johnnie Gilhooley of Cowdenbeath, could leave three defenders trailing in his wake with one feint. Even at sixteen he was developing that famous arrogant strut. He was often in my notebook as one of the inevitable "three best for Crossgates...", and Baxter even today confesses how thrilled he was to see his name mentioned in these reports.

In 1957, Jim was asked to play a trial for Raith Rovers, the biggest of the Fife clubs at that time. First, he had to get the permission of Mick Johnston, the hard under-manager at Fordell Colliery, to leave his shift early on the Saturday.

"After the shift on the Wednesday, I joined the queue waiting to see Mick. I could hear the older miners exchanging swear-words and other assorted insults. This was the time when you made complaints or asked for favours. Mick was not known for listening with a sympathetic ear to either.

"In fact, when I look back, I'm fairly sure there were times when he didn't listen at all. So when it was my turn to put a case for what was called an 'early tow' up the pit, Mick was in an even less receptive mood than usual. You had the impression that to ask him for a favour was a bit like patting a crocodile. 'Aye,' he said. 'What do you want, then?'

"You must understand that when he asked that question, he put it slightly more colourfully, but we needn't go into that. I explained that I needed a line to finish at twelve that Saturday.

'What fur?'

'Well, I've got this trial for Raith Rovers and....'

'A trial for Raith Rovers! You! It's a plate of porridge you need.'

"He might have been right at that, considering that I still didn't weigh enough to go out in a high wind.

'What's your name?'

'Eh, well, Jim Baxter.'

He leaned back and stared at me again. 'So you're Jim Baxter. Aye, well.'

"It was then that I realised that any reputation I was gaining for playing football could come in handy. Mick had actually heard of me. To be honest, I was quite pleased. I realised, too, the grip football can have on a pit community. Mick may have been an under-manager, but he was still a mining man. He gave me my line. He didn't exactly wish me luck, but I suspect he thought about it. It might have made him sound weak, though, the last thing he could afford."

So Jim came up the pit that Saturday at noon instead of half past one, and went straight home for a wash and a dinner of mince and tatties. He played against a Rangers reserve side which included the likes of Johnny Valentine, Don Kichenbrand, Ralph Brand, Jimmy Millar and Davy Wilson. Raith signed Baxter after the match, offering a weekly wage of £3. If he got into the first team, he would earn £9 a week, £2 more than his pit wage.

Jim Baxter had found his way out of the pit prison.

"Nobody likes going down the pit," he says. "Nobody gets up in the morning full of enthusiasm at the prospect of another shift. A man becomes a miner partly through tradition, and partly because it's often the only job going. There is never any other reason that makes sense. Whenever I hear the comfortably-off talk

148

about miners with mortgages and motorcars, as if they were just like superior bank clerks who happened to get their hands dirty, I feel like asking a few questions. Like....why don't you try it for yourself, some time?"

Baxter played for Raith for three seasons along with players such as Willie McNaught, Willie Polland and Johnny Urquhart. He had hoped that his idols, Hibs, might sign him, but Rangers paid £27,000 for his signature. His basic wage would be £22 per week, with a £3 bonus for a win.

Jim soon became the darling of the Rangers fans, especially when he arrogantly tormented Celtic. He was soon capped for Scotland. He was a star in Scotland's defeat of the Auld Enemy, England, at Hampden in 1962, and the following year he scored two goals in Scotland's victory over England at Wembley. But the match which stands out in most Scots' memories must be the 3-2 victory over England at Wembley on April 15, 1967 – known as 'Baxter's international'. England had just won the World Cup, and had played nineteen games without defeat. They were expected to beat Scotland comfortably.

Jim Baxter ran the game, with an effortless, virtuoso performance which is unlikely ever to be equalled. When the Scots were ahead, Baxter played 'keepy-uppy' on his own, and even sat on the ball, daring people to tackle him. Dark blue jersey flapping outside his brief shorts, he would put his foot on the ball, then walk away from it as if he were bored. The English supporters could have killed him. As Stuart Cosgrove put it: "He acted out all the schoolboy fantasies, weaving his way past English defenders with consummate ease, beckoning them to take the ball with gestures of smug superiority, scoring now and again, and sitting on the ball when being brilliant became a bore. It was national absolution: they won the World Cup but we played football." How Hooky would have savoured that!

The ghost of Hooky Leonard certainly hovered around Baxter's off-the-field exploits. He was Scotland's first pop football superstar, and he dressed the part. He revelled in the high life.

"My old pals from Fife would come over quite regularly, and we'd go to all the best night spots. The best that we knew, anyway. My picture was in the papers almost every day, and if they weren't calling me a superstar, they were calling me a playboy. I didn't much mind either, to be honest. And my mates couldn't believe their luck. Their eyes would pop almost out of their heads, as we walked into, say, La Ronde in Sauchiehall Street, where good-looking birds were wall to wall. 'Take it easy,' I'd say, real man of the world stuff. 'Don't chase them, they'll be over.' And they were.

"Of course, I was still learning. At 21 I didn't know much about anything. The 21-year-olds of today are far more mature. I was still more of a boy than a man. So far as food was concerned, fish and chips or steak and eggs were all right with me, and table wine was a closed book. There weren't too many restaurants in Cowdenbeath where you could ask for the claret to be served at room temperature, please."

The invasion of the Cowdenbeath playboys is one of the more touching episodes of recent Scottish football history, perhaps making up for the indignities Cowdenbeath Football Club had suffered at the hands of the West of Scotland football mafia over many years. Baxter would install the West Fife miners in a salubrious Glasgow hotel, and arrange outrageous drinking parties. The bills were sent to Ibrox, and the club paid up, with gritted teeth. Their playboy superstar was too much of a crowd puller to risk offending him.

Jim loved tormenting the footballing authorities even more than he loved tormenting defenders. At the end of the Scottish Cup final replay in 1963 in which Rangers beat Celtic 3-0, Baxter grabbed the ball, stuffed it up his jersey, and waddled off the pitch like a very pregnant woman. Despite referee Tiny Wharton's attempts to get the ball, Baxter kept it and gave it to Ian McMillan, who was about to retire from football.

Willie Allan, the SFA secretary, who Baxter nicknamed 'Oor Wullie' and pilloried as "a pompous pain in the neck", wrote to Rangers demanding the return of the ball – "and if it doesn't turn up we will take steps to ensure that it does. If we ignore the business, it would be a case of the law of the jungle taking over."

A football was returned to the SFA, but was it the football in question? Ask Jim Baxter.

Although Baxter was much wealthier than he would have been

had he stayed down the mines, he was very poor compared to the superstars of today, many of whom could not lace the Cowdenbeath man's boots. Today, a Rangers internationalist may get a signing on fee of several hundred thousand pounds, and a weekly wage of £2000 plus, as well as promotional spinoffs. Several of the top players in Britain today are millionaires. In 1965, while acknowledged to be a world-class player at the peak of his powers, Jim Baxter's weekly wage was £45. He asked for a transfer, and Rangers, fed up with shelling out thousands of pounds for Baxter's extra-mural activities, transferred him to Sunderland for £80,000. Baxter's share was £11,000, and his basic weekly wage rose to £80. From Sunderland he moved to Nottingham Forest for £100,000, but by this time his lifestyle was taking a heavy toll. He was given a free transfer in 1969 and returned to Rangers, but within a year he was out of the game at the early age of 30. In 1969 he was picked up by the police after allegedly driving under the influence of drink in Cowdenbeath after a Cowdenbeath v. Rangers friendly match. He was fined £25 and banned from driving for a year. A player of Baxter's class could have gone on at the top level for a few more years, but he hadn't taken sufficient care of himself for that to be possible. He bought a pub near Ibrox, but after a few years that venture failed. His admitted drinking and gambling – he estimated having lost about £200,000 since first going to Rangers – meant that he had little to show for his time at the top.

Except memories. And what memories!

******

January, 1993. The first game of the New Year is postponed because of the bad weather.

The attack on the Cowdenbeath board continues in the columns of the local paper.

"This is the worst Cowdenbeath team to be seen at Central Park for many a year," writes one local. "The team that John Brownlie and Gordon Miller built up is slowly being decimated. Only Mr McDougall knows why he chose to sack Mr Brownlie and chase Mr Miller away. Mr McDougall then appointed Andy Harrow as manager, probably on the cheap, like everything else at

Central Park.

"Why did he choose to decimate the team, and sell the club, players and supporters down the river? I think the supporters have a better idea, Mr McDougall. Sell the club and get out among your stock car friends."

The letter closes with a call to former chairman Tom Currie to take over the club again.

January 9, 1993. Partick Thistle 0, Cowdenbeath 1.

The sensation of the Scottish Cup! Cowdenbeath, anchored at the bottom of the First Division, with the worst defensive record in Britain, travel to Premier League Partick Thistle's Firhill ground, with all the experts forecasting a cricket score for Thistle.

The game begins with Cowdenbeath surprisingly on the attack. This is not in the script. Eddie Petrie runs from his own penalty area into the Thistle goalmouth, and is thwarted at the crucial moment. Then Tom Condie nips in while the Partick defence hesitates, and lobs just over the bar. In 36 minutes Condie again beats the Thistle defence but his shot hits the post and runs along the Partick goal line! Unsettled by Cowdenbeath's attacking surges, Thistle gradually come back into the game, but Billy Lamont is in fine form in goal for Cowdenbeath.

The second half begins with Cowdenbeath on the attack again. Willie Callaghan is through on goal when he is brought down by goalkeeper Nelson. Nicky Henderson keeps his nerve, and puts the ball into the net from the penalty spot. Thistle go into panic mode, and start pumping high balls into the Cowdenbeath goal area. The Cowdenbeath defence, with central defender Hugh Douglas playing with a broken nose and stitches in his eye, stands firm.

In 56 minutes, Partick are awarded a penalty when Robertson brings down Shaw. McVicar steps up to take the kick, but the confident Lamont is not going to be beaten by anyone today. He dives to save. The keeper is mobbed by his jubilant team mates. The last few minutes are agony for the Blue Brazil supporters, especially as the game moves into injury time, but Cowden hold out to win the match. Billy Lamont is made the sponsors' Man of the Match, a decision no one can disagree with.

The result makes the television headlines. Partick's embarrassment is acute. Andy Harrow says of his players: "They were all heroes as far as I am concerned. The last time we played as a team like we did on Saturday, we won at Ayr. Admittedly, we got a few of the breaks we have not been getting in the league, but the players worked for these breaks. If we play like this in the league, we can still make a comeback."

Is this the breakthrough for which the Cowdenbeath fans have been yearning? Is 1993 going to bring better fortune?

Cowdenbeath are drawn at home to Premier league club Hibernian in the next round of the Cup.

In the evening I phone the Reverend Erik Cramb, one of the fellowship of ecclesiastical nutters, who supports Partick Thistle. I sense tears on the line. He who has for years been condescending to me in the way that only a Thistle man can be to a Cowdenbeath supporter, is close to the edge.

I try to keep before me the pastoral nature of such a conversation. I try to remind myself that Christianity is essentially a religion of mercy. I try to keep a triumphal note out of my voice.

I fail I fail I fail.

And, oh, what enjoyment there is in the failing.

January 20: Cowdenbeath 2, Meadowbank 2.

Henderson and Condie give Cowden a two goal lead, but the old defensive frailties show themselves again. Another late goal gives Meadowbank a share of the points.

January 27: Cowdenbeath 0, St Mirren 3

Cowden simply fail to compete. Relegation is now virtually a certainty. It is only a matter of when.

The only thing to look forward to now is a Scottish Cup date with Hibernian.

Dream on.

February

These detective stories on TV always end at precisely the right moment – after the criminal is arrested and before the court turns him loose – Robert Orben

You're very deceptive, son. You're even slower than you look – Tommy Docherty, manager, to one of his players.

'GET FINDLAY' is the cry amongst Scotland's criminal fraternity: for Donald Findlay, QC, is quite simply the best criminal advocate in Scotland.

He is also from Cowdenbeath. But he has torn up the script: he is a high Tory, an Egyptologist, and vice chairman of Rangers Football Club.

Claret-drinking Tory Egyptologists from Cowdenbeath are, one has to say, an endangered species. In fact, only one has ever been spotted. But Donald Findlay is no ordinary man.

Born in Cowdenbeath in 1951, Donald comes of mining stock by way of his maternal grandfather. His paternal grandfather owned a newsagent/tobacconists. His father, James, was, among other things, an inspector on the buses and a church beadle.

Donald Findlay, Q.C., outside the High Court, Edinburgh

Donald lived at 121 High Street, Cowdenbeath and attended Lumphinnans Primary School. When he was nine years old, his family moved to the new town of Glenrothes, before going to live in Dundee. His education continued at Harris Academy, Dundee, and then Dundee University, where he graduated in 1973 with a first class honours degree in Scots law. He gained the degree of Master of Philosophy at Glasgow University, and was admitted to the Faculty of Advocates in 1975. He took silk to become Queen's Counsel in 1988.

From early days he had wanted to be a criminal lawyer.

"It all goes back to the Fifties when there was a programme on television called Boyd QC," he recalls. "I was fascinated by it. There was something very appealing about this guy who was always taking on the forces of adversity, albeit they were theoretically the good guys and he was representing the bad guys."

Donald Findlay has been involved in the defence in many major criminal trials in recent times – the 'ice cream war' murders in Glasgow; the trial of Paul Ferris in 1992 for the murder of the son of Glasgow gangland boss Arthur Thomson; and more recently in the two cases attracting publicity because of "not proven" verdicts – the murder of the Greenock taxi driver and the murder of Amanda Jane Duffy in Hamilton; most recently in the successful defence of Daniel Boyle, the first man in Scotland to be tried twice for the same murder. He also successfully defended a man accused of murdering a drug runner, by pointing out that his client had actually shot the man when he was already dead, which he claimed was not a criminal offence under Scots law. He has a superb track record for a leading defence counsel.

Findlay's brilliant forensic skills and commanding, theatrical presence – with mutton-chop sideburns and Sherlock Holmes pipe, he is not a man to be ignored – make him the first choice for anyone facing life imprisonment.

In 1989 he was adopted as prospective Conservative Party candidate for Cunninghame North. The battle with sitting M.P. Brian Wilson was much looked forward to, but Findlay withdrew due to pressure of work.

Was it not unusual for a man brought up in a mining community like Cowdenbeath to be a leading light in the Tory party?

Donald Findlay's politics were shaped by his father, who raged against what he saw as the Labour party's condescension towards working people. James Findlay's only son's political views are quite straightforward.

"The Labour party treats people with contempt," he says, vehemently. "Even as a child I couldn't understand why people were labelled as working-class, middle-class or whatever. We didn't look on ourselves as working-class, or any kind of class. We were just us."

His upbringing certainly helped him communicate with all kinds of people, including those from very tough backgrounds.

"I hope I can get on with most of them because I talk their language. I don't talk down to them. I don't talk like an Edinburgh lawyer to them. If I have a point to make I'll make it bluntly, and yes, I suspect this is unusual. I've had solicitors tell me 'you'll get nothing out of him', and within fifteen minutes we'll be chatting away. That pleases me."

And Egyptology? Was it the coal bings of Cowdenbeath that reminded him of the pyramids?

"I've always been interested in ancient Egypt, but it was really brought home to me one night during a sound and light show at the pyramids. It was supremely well done. So many thousands of years on, people are still talking about the pharaohs.That must be the nearest thing to immortality that you can have."

Donald Findlay played football as a child in Cowdenbeath, and played rugby at Harris Academy. He was asked to join the board of Rangers Football Club in 1991, and became vice chairman the following year.

"I was delighted to accept the invitation," he says. "Obviously as an avid bluenose in your heart of hearts you thought that maybe one day you could, maybe, get on to the Ibrox board, but really you never ever thought that the chance would come."

He has been a Rangers supporter since boyhood – "but have always retained a great affection for Cowdenbeath, the town and the football club," he reassures me.

This extraordinary Cowdenbeath graduate could be handy. Maybe he could get some free training gear from Ibrox for the hard-up Blue Brazilians, or some supplies for the "board room" in the portakabin.

Or maybe he could save a man in his hour of extremity, as he faces a hostile mob baying for his blood.

Keep his number by your phone, Mr Harrow. Remember: Get Findlay.

Get Harrow. That's the bloodcurdling message from the disenchanted terraces. The manager is barracked every game by unhappy fans who are increasingly embarrassed by the team's miserable performances.

Cowdenbeath are the joke team of Scotland. What is hardest for the fans to take is the ridicule from Dunfermline. The Auld Enemy are already opening the skylight window which will take them back up into the Premier league, while Cowdenbeath are all but through the trap door leading back down to oblivion.

It's not Andy Harrow's fault that John Brownlie left in such unhappy circumstances. It's not his fault that he has no money to spend on players. It's not his fault that he is facing this crisis with so little managerial experience behind him. But he has to endure the taunts from the terracing, and it's not easy. The beleaguered manager is in the middle of a personal nightmare.

In a full-page spread titled COWDEN-GRIEF in *Scottish Football,* he opens his heart on the problems of bossing what the magazine describes as "the worst team in Britain". He talks about his own disillusionment with some of the players under his care.

"There are too many bad professionals in the game at the moment," he says, "people who are only in the game to pick up a bit of money and just aren't interested in improving as players. They come up with too many excuses to miss training. Everyone here thinks they should be in the team all the time, and it causes huge problems if they are not in one week.

"They all assume that they're better than the guy that's taken their place, but they never actually look at themselves and think that they might not be playing as well as they could be.

"There are loads of secret meetings between different groups of players. They all want to have a moan about something or other. And if I speak to an individual player in private about something, nine times out of ten he'll walk straight out and tell everyone else what's been said anyway. That's not on.

"Most of the players here have only ever played in the Second Division or in the Juniors, but they assume they know it all. A lot of them got a shock at the step-up in standard from the Second to the First Division, and, to be quite honest, some of them aren't good enough."

The Cowdenbeath manager talks about the decline in morale caused by continuous defeats.

"Confidence is defintely low and, as a consequence, what were small problems seem to be getting bigger and bigger. Because the stand burned down, we've had to change in portakabins, which no one is very happy about, but it seems to be getting moaned about more and more as the defeats mount up. It's not easy for the players when you run out in front of a few hundred people and hardly get a cheer. That really kills morale.

"Sometimes I go home on a Saturday night, sit down and think that maybe I am getting it wrong, but it never lasts long. I do think I'm doing the right thing at the club, but it's sometimes difficult to ignore the stick that I get from the fans. I've dropped some of their favourites who won them promotion for the first time in twenty years, but I believe in what I'm doing.

"But I've made mistakes, and plenty of them. I've picked the wrong teams and the wrong tactics, but it's my first job and you have to learn from your mistakes. Everyone from the chairman, the secretary and me through to the players is a bit new to the game at this level, and we could use someone with a bit of experience just to give us a bit of guidance."

Does he get depressed and feel like quitting?

"The only time I don't look forward to the next game is on a Saturday night after we've lost. The rest of the week I can fight against the feelings of gloom and I end up looking forward to our matches on a Saturday. I keep believing that one good result on a Saturday could turn it around for is. That keeps me going."

Feelings of gloom? The manager of Cowdenbeath? Quelle Surprise, as they say in Lochgelly. Or Jamphlars.

February 2, 1993: Morton 3, Cowdenbeath 2
Yet again, a game is lost in the final ten minutes. Goals from

Robertson and Wright put Cowdenbeath ahead, but the defence crumbles again near the end.

It looks ominous for Saturday's Scottish Cup tie against Premier league side Hibernian. The media are full of stories ridiculing Cowdenbeath for their leaking Portakabins and their leaking defence.

February 6: Cowdenbeath 0, Hibernian 0.

The big-time returns to Central Park. As with the Partick Thistle game, Cowdenbeath harry and fight, and defend really well. Willie Lamont is once again a hero in goal, making several spectacular saves. The Cowdenbeath supporters in the 4,509 crowd give the team strong vocal backing, and the players respond with a whole-hearted display.

There is drama two minutes from the end when Billy Herd is brought down by a despairing Gordon Hunter tackle as he moves through with only the goalkeeper to beat. It is a clear penalty (confirmed that evening on television), but referee Joe Timmons waves the protesting Cowdenbeath players away. What a sensational finish to the cup tie it would have been!

After the game, a proud Andy Harrow comments: "I thought that we defended brilliantly against Hibs, with Willie Lamont outstanding, along with the three centre backs. And I thought we should have had a penalty. Everyone played their part, and I was delighted with the reaction of the fans. Their backing was great."

A friend writes to me: "Cowdenbeath's problem is obvious. They are really a Premier league side."

February 10: Hibernian 1, Cowdenbeath 0.

8,701 fans watch Hibs squeeze through at Easter Road. Cowdenbeath again defend well, and give the home side some anxious moments. It is another gutsy performance by the Cowdenbeath players, who are given a standing ovation by their fans at the end of the game.

Now, another long-awaited game against the Auld Enemy.

February 13: Cowdenbeath 1, Dunfermline 2.

Paul Smith gives Dunfermline the lead in 38 minutes, and

Nicky Henderson equalises five minutes after the interval. Cowdenbeath are making a real game of it when Billy Herd is sent off after elbowing visiting defender Neale Cooper. Scott Leitch gives the Pars victory with a goal in 72 minutes.

February 17: Stirling Albion 2, Cowdenbeath 1.
Yet another goal in the last ten minutes sinks Cowden.

February 20: Kilmarnock 1, Cowdenbeath 1.
Cowdenbeath battle well, and shock promotion-seeking Kilmarnock with a Henderson goal in 54 minutes. The game goes deep into injury time, with the Cowdenbeath fans believing a sensational victory has been achieved. A shot bounces from Willie Lamont's chest, and Callum Campbell scores with the rebound.

February 23: Cowdenbeath 0, Dumbarton 2.
Willie Lamont, hero of so many big games, absentmindedly picks up a ball outside the penalty area, giving the Sons an indirect free kick. Lamont inexplicably hands the ball to the inrushing McQuade, who quickly passes to McAneny before the Cowdenbeath defence has regrouped. The freak goal demoralises Cowden. Yet another late goal finishes them off.

February 27: Cowdenbeath 0, Raith Rovers 2.
"I thought the recipe was there for another good show by the boys," says Andy Harrow. "After all, they were playing at home in front of a big crowd and against the league leaders. But they put on a strangely subdued performance and it was all rather disappointing."

What is probably even more disappointing is the defeat of the Cowdenbeath youth team 1-0 by Montrose in the quarter final of the BP Youth Cup, after extra time. The youngsters had done remarkably well to reach the latter stages of the tournament, and had high hopes of advancing to the semi final.

It is announced that the Cowdenbeath youngsters will go to Sweden in the summer to play in a summer youth tournament.

Andy Harrow turns out for the Cowdenbeath reserves, and scores a goal. He denies that he is planning a comeback.

March

Lots of times managers have to be cheats and conmen. We are the biggest hypocrites. We cheat. The only way to survive is by cheating. – Tommy Docherty.

Progress may have been all right but it has gone on too long. – Ogden Nash.

DREAM. DREAM. What will happen when Cowdenbeath Football Club sort out their present temporary troubles, spring into the Premier league, and return to their rightful place in Europe?
Return?
You laugh because you do not understand.
Unlike many of the lumpen clubs in the Scottish leagues, Cowdenbeath have a good European pedigree. In fact, they taught the Germans how to play football. Cowdenbeath FC rank among the aristocrats of Europe.
Cowden's first venture into Europe was in 1925, after their first season in the First Division. Having finished fifth in the league, just behind Celtic, they were rightly regarded as one of Scotland's most attractive sides. At the end of that successful season, they set sail for Gibraltar. Most of the team were sick throughout the journey, the worst afflicted being their Scottish international goalkeeper John Falconer.
Their first game was against the army stationed at the rock. Willie Devlin ran riot, scoring two goals, the other scorers being Hooky Leonard, Andy Rankin and Porky Chambers. Yes, Porky.
After a Sunday afternoon at a bullfight, a rumour swept through Cowdenbeath to the effect that the team had been wiped out in a road accident. Cowdenbeath's next victories were 6-1, 5-1 and 2-0, with Willie Devlin becoming a hero because of his mazy dribbling skills. Hooky Leonard became another idol, especially

when Cowden destroyed a Seville select in Cadiz.

Three years later, Germany was the destination. Cowdenbeath had been invited to play some exhibition matches, and show some of the finer points of soccer to the German nation. The club captain, Willie Rankin, sent regular despatches back home to the local Cowdenbeath paper.

"The party," he wrote in a style which suggested that he was translating from German in his head, "entered into the proper spirit of the tour, each one trying to make the experience as pleasant as possible for one another. Stories and singing whiled away the time in the train until bedtime, and then the spirit of socialism set in so strong that the players did not see why the directors should have pillows and they should have none. So a raid took place, and the players were triumphant as they bore off the spoils of the campaign in the form of pillows.

"The sea journey was not so enjoyable – for some. Falconer was about the first to go to the side of the ship, and just as lunch was served, others went to join him."

Then, on to the night clubs of Cologne.

"The shows were very good, with the drawback that none of the party could speak German. Davie Moyes tried it on the waiters who, he discovered, could talk English better than he could himself."

On to Nuremburg, by boat – "the journey down the Rhine valley was exceedingly beautiful, and the players were all so impressed that they stated it was nearly as beautiful as Scotland, but not quite." John Falconer failed to appreciate the beauty: he would have exchanged his wavy view of the Black Forest for a toe-hold on a subsiding street in Cowdenbeath surrounded by bings.

More than twenty thousand specators crammed into the Nuremberg sports stadium for Cowdenbeath's first match of the European tour against a select team from all over Germany.

The start was ominous.

"When I went to toss the coin," wrote the Cowdenbeath captain, "there was neither head nor tail. Nobody could speak English, but I tossed the coin. No person there spoke a word. When the coin came down, the referee awarded the choice of ends to our opponents – sort of 'heads I win, tails you lose' stuff. The referee and linesmen – there are four linesmen, one in each half of the field – were one-sided, allowing the Olympic team to push and kick even when the ball was away from you. After the first half hour, when the referee started to go in their favour, they took advantage of it and hashed and kicked us all over the park, and if anyone retaliated they were told about it. They played the better football, although Cowdenbeath were at a disadvantage in everything – first, the hot night; then the ball was much smaller than we play with at home.

"The referee was very unkind. His decisions were awful, and completely broke the hearts and spirits of the Scotch boys. The centre-half of the Olympic team was actually telling the referee what to do."

Herr Willy von Miller?

The small ball went once past the perpetually sick-as-a-parrot John Falconer without reply from the "Scotch boys", who were glad simply to walk off the pitch at the end.

Next stop, Munich. Another sail, this time through the Bavarian Alps: then on to a local beer hall – "some of the boys did some dancing, and Flannigan gave an exhibition of the 'Black Bottom', which was enjoyed by all."

The game was not so enjoyable. A 4-2 defeat. Then Leipzig. 8-2 for the Germans. Berlin for a break: then on to the mining district of Dortmund for the final game of the tour in front of forty thousand fans. German Olympic Select 5, Cowdenbeath 1. Willie Rankin's verdict:

"Of course, they are typical Germans; they must win by fair means or foul. In our last match they got three goals which were ridiculous. At home they would have been instantly chalked off, but what can we do? It was the same referee, and we had no chance, although there was less pushing. I think we have taught them not to, and they have taken their lesson well, for they cut it out quite a lot.

"The German team, although not very good sports on the field, are fine fellows when off it, and before they left the field they gave Cowdenbeath three cheers. We then had coffee with them and spent a pleasant hour in their company.

"Speeches were made first by the secretary of the German Association, and then by a reporter who spoke English. He thanked the Cowdenbeath club for their kindness in coming from Scotland – the motherland of football – to Germany to let them see how the game was played there. On behalf of the German public, clubs and players, he thanked all, and hoped the Scottish team would again visit the land. He then called on the Olympic players to show their heartfelt thanks, which were shown by three hearty cheers."

Mr Preston, one of the Cowdenbeath directors, replied on behalf of the club.

"He expressed the feelings of all of us (Cowdenbeath) in a nice little speech, finishing up by hoping that some day he would see the German teams taking their place among the teams of the world, for they were very apt pupils. He was glad that they had picked on Scotland for their opponents for the Olympic team test, for he was quite sure that they could get no better teachers of football than the Scots. Mr Scott Duncan then called for three hearty cheers, which were given by the visitors, followed by the singing of 'For they are jolly good fellows.'"

Apt pupils indeed. 1-0, 4-2, 8-2, 5-1.

All that remained was the journey home – by sea.

Ach, well.

* * * * * * *

So how did Cowdenbeath do in their last little venture into the higher reaches of Scottish football? The 1970/71 season – their first in the First Division proper since 1934 (apart from five games in the abortive 1939/40 season) – was not a glorious one. Cowdenbeath simply didn't have the depth of player pool to overcome serious injuries to a number of key players. Three first team members sustained broken legs, and keeper Alan Wylie's career ended in a car crash. Cowdenbeath won only one game at home, and spent most of the season firmly anchored at the bottom of the league. They finished there with only 17 points.

The season was not without its bright spots. Cowden reached the League Cup semi finals, losing 2-0 to Rangers at Hampden. Eighteen-year-old goalkeeper Jim McArthur, who had made his debut for Cowdenbeath at the age of 15, was introduced towards the end of the season, and showed excellent form. What pleased the fans most, though, was that Cowden beat Dunfermline on each of the four times they met, and won the Fife Cup for the first time in 36 years by beating the Pars in both legs of the final. Kings of Kingdom of Fife!

Back in the old familiar Second Division, Cowdenbeath almost bounced straight back. Only a 2-0 defeat by Arbroath in the last game of the season prevented them from returning to the First Division. Then, back to the old familiar financial crisis. Billy Mullen moved to Hong Kong, Andy Kinnell was transferred to St Johnstone, the promising young full back Billy McLaughlan was killed in an accident, John Dickson was transferred to St Mirren and Jim McArthur was sold to Hibs. Soon thereafter Jim Taylor moved to St Mirren, Davy Ross to St Johnstone, and promising striker Andy Harrow to Raith Rovers. Billy Bostock, Cowdenbeath's leading postwar goalscorer with 72 goals to his credit, was freed. The bank manager was happy, but the team plunged down the League.

Andy Matthew resigned as manager in September 1974, having done a superb job for the club. He had produced an attractive, attacking side which, when it was not in the First Division, was always challenging for promotion. He was one of the most successful managers in the club's history, but at the end of the day he was defeated by the need to sell his most successful players in order to keep the creditors at bay. It was ever thus.

Matthew's departure signalled a period of tremendous instability within Cowdenbeath Football Club. Andy was succeeded by Bert Paton, who lasted only a few weeks before being followed by Dan McLindon. He was in post for a year, with Frank Connor succeeding him. Two years later Connor moved to Raith Rovers and Pat Wilson took over. In 1980, there was another change of manager when Pat Stanton occupied the hot seat, but within weeks he was on his way to Dunfermline. Former Cowdenbeath player Andy Rolland took over.

A local boy, Andy had first signed for Cowdenbeath in 1961. He played six games at centre forward, but was freed at the end of the season. When Archie Robertson became manager in 1964, he re-signed Rolland, whom he had coached in the local Boys'

Brigade team. Robertson moved him into midfield and then to left back, and when right back Bobby Wilson was transferred to Dundee, Andy took over his berth. His powerful running and shooting won him many admirers, and in 1967 he was transferred to Dundee United for £10,000. He played at Tannadice for eleven years, and was capped by the Scottish League.

In 1978, Rolland was appointed player-manager of Dunfermline Athletic. In the last game of the season, with Dunfermline requiring one point to be promoted, Andy equalised from the penalty spot. After a short time in the First Division, club and player fell out over payments, and Rolland moved to Central Park for the third time.

Spurred on by their new boss, Cowdenbeath challenged strongly for promotion. In the last game of the season, Cowden, like Dunfermline before them, needed a point to go up. A penalty was awarded, and Rolland stepped up again. He missed – his first failure from the penalty spot in six years – and Cowden remained in the Second Division. Rolland resigned in 1982 (at the age of forty he was reinstated to the junior ranks and continued to play for several seasons).

Hugh Wilson succeeded Rolland on the managerial merry-go-round, and a year later Willie McCulloch was manager. Another year on, and former Lisbon Lion John Clark was in charge.

Clark brought order to the club, and built a useful side which almost won promotion. The best players in the team then had to be sold. Jim Liddle, Kenny Ward and Billy Blackie moved to Forfar, Craig Levein to Hearts, Grant Tierney to Meadowbank, Colin McGlashan to Clyde, Scottish Under 21 player Jim Marshall to Raith Rovers, Derek Grant to Airdrie, David Shanks to Clydebank and Roddy Grant to St Johnstone.

Everything was changing. It was symbolised by the removal of the last remaining image of Cowdenbeath as a mining community with the closure of British Coal's Central Workshops and officers, built on the site of Cowdenbeath Football Club's first ground.

The only permanent fixture during this turbulent period was goalkeeper Ray Allan who, having made his debut for Cowdenbeath in 1972, went on to attain the club record of 489 League and Cup appearances.

In 1987 Dick Campbell was appointed manager, with John Blackley following him through the revolving Cowdenbeath door a matter of weeks later. In 1988 John Brownlie became Cowdenbeath's thirteenth manager in fourteen years.

Brownlie was to be the club's longest serving manager since Andy Matthew. And the most successful. Just before he was sacked.

For they are jolly good fellows.

Ach, well.

* * * * *

Well, how is Cowden's first season in the First Division since 1970/71 going?

March 6, 1993. Ayr United 3, Cowdenbeath 1.

Surprise, surprise. Two goals in the last five minutes finish Cowden off.

The only question now is: will Cowdenbeath be the first team in Britain to be relegated this season?

March 9. Clydebank 5, Cowdenbeath 0.

Can the season be called to an end now, please?

March 13. Cowdenbeath 1, Stirling Albion 1.

If Cowdenbeath had lost this one, they would have been officially relegated. Billy Herd scored with one minute left, thus delaying the inevitable.

March 20. Meadowbank Thistle 3, Cowdenbeath 1.

Down, and out. Cowdenbeath are the first British club side to be relegated this season.

Andy Harrow says: "We have to start planning now for the new season. I will not be keeping players who do not want to give their all for the club."

Gordon McDougall decides to answer the deluge of criticism from the terracing and in the correspondence columns of the *Central Fife Times*. The directors still stand accused of having little interest in the club's future, and of only being interested in stock car racing – an accusation that has haunted them all season.

The manager stands accused of bringing substandard players to the club and of using the wrong tactics for matches.

In an open letter to the Cowdenbeath fans, who feel badly let down by a season of embarrassments, the club chairman confirms that Andy Harrow will be staying on as manager, and emphasises the board's view that the development of a youth policy is the only way forward for the club. He also reveals that he has had thoughts of quitting.

"Over the thirty months that I have been connected with Cowdenbeath Football Club," the chairman writes, "last Saturday's game against Stirling Albion saw the first time that the thought crossed my mind that I had wasted my time and money in saving the club from certain extinction. The thought struck home after approximately ten minutes when a section of the crowd, with the score at 0-0, started barracking manager Andy Harrow, myself and the board. I have no objection to football fans who pay their hard earned money to attend games being entitled to voice their feelings. As a keen fan, I have done that myself in the past.

"What really sickens me is the subjects they choose to focus their feelings on, namely Andy Harrow, their claim that myself and the board are only interested in stock cars; and their solution to the problems, sack the manager and go out and spend money on players. I feel these points are totally unjustified.

"Let me say that Andy Harrow, at a particularly volatile time for the club due to promotion, became our new manager with no money available for new players, and no office or changing rooms to work with, other than portakabins. All these things were forced upon him, and his position has never been discussed, as we firmly believe that he has not had the chance anyone is entitled to expect."

Mr McDougall goes on to argue that far from being the problem, it is actually the stock car racing which keeps Cowdenbeath Football Club afloat.

"The boys who hurl the abuse didn't have to sweet-talk officials from the Gas Board or Electricity Board from cutting off supplies; pay for new floodlighting because the club couldn't afford to after instructing the job to go ahead; try to stop the sheriff officers from poinding valuable football equipment because VAT payments were habitually late; or even stop a joiner taking back the front door he had fitted as it hadn't been paid for. I faced all these things and many more before making my successful offer for the shares of the club in 1990.

"Despite letters which have appeared in local newspapers suggesting differently, without myself being in the right place at the right time, there would be no Cowdenbeath Football Club today. Unless, that is, some other benefactor had come along.

"Through careful use of what funds have been available, debts of close to £250,000 have been reduced and secured to the extent that we can now face the bank manager and there are no creditors breathing down our neck for payment.

"I am no millionaire. What I make I have to work damned hard for and also long hours, and having seen the position a football club can get into by living outwith its means, I have no intention of ever letting Cowdenbeath sink to that level again."

Having got that off his chest, the beleaguered chairman then goes on to the offensive.

"My message to the 'Harrow and McDougall brigade must go' is this. The manager, myself and the other directors dislike being beaten every week just as much as you do, but unfortunately, there is no easy answer. For next season there might, if the deals are right, be some players signed via the transfer market, there may be other bits of wheeling and dealing, but the real future of the club lies in only one direction, and that is via our youth set-up. The problem is that it takes time, and that is where those same fans who are after our blood just now can play their part. Despite your frustrations at the moment, there are good young players at the club. The present atmosphere is, however, crucifying them. It's the old story of a bit of barracking from a ten thousand crowd goes practically unheard, but when there are only two or three hundred, every comment goes home.

"Give the team your support over the remaining games, if only for the sake of these kids. If you feel you can't manage this, I'd rather not be accused of taking your money.

"One final point. The directors and myself have, since we took over, taken not one penny out of the club. One of our early board decisions was that no director would be paid for any work done

169

for the club. Crazy as it may seem, we see it as a labour of love!"

March 27. Cowdenbeath 0, Hamilton 4.
Kenny Ward, the player most Cowdenbeath fans would like to see back at Central Park according to a poll of the fans, scores a hat-trick against his old club. The attendance is a miserable 239, the smallest crowd at a senior game in Britain that day.

Cowdenbeath Football Club make a private settlement with former manager John Brownlie on the day the industrial tribunal is due to resume. Mr Brownlie, and directors Tom Currie and James Marshall, are due to give evidence.

The joint statement does not disclose the terms of the settlement and forbids either party from making any further statements.

"Cowdenbeath FC and their former manager, John Brownlie have agreed to settle the outstanding matters between them on a private basis," reads the statement. "This is done without any admission of liability on the part of the club."

Question: Would the total settlement costs have secured John Brownlie's future with the club back in May? If so, would there have only been 239 fans at Central Park for a First Division game in March with six weeks of the season still to run? Would the total legal costs of the boardroom battles and the Brownlie case have bought a couple of the kind of players the manager wanted?

Experience, they say, is the name we give to our mistakes.

April

My son was born to play for Scotland. He has all the qualities — a massive ego, a criminal record, an appalling drink problem. And he's not very good at football. – Mrs Alice Cosgrove

The louder he talked of his honour, the faster we counted our spoons. – Ralph Waldo Emerson

APRIL 3, 1993. Dumbarton 0, Cowdenbeath 0.
A brilliant display in goal by young Alan Combe saves Cowdenbeath from the embarrassment of losing their 100th goal of the season.

A Cowdenbeath supporter, signing himself 'Angry ex-fan', replies to Gordon McDougall in the *Central Fife Times*.
"Well done, Mr McDougall. How clever you are to save Cowdenbeath from extinction. You seem to have overlooked the fact that you and your directors are totally responsible for the club's current crisis. Let's just get the facts straight –
1. You sacked a perfectly good manager because of personality differences.
2. If you had loved the club so much, you would have taken proper steps to ensure First Division survival. You did things on the cheap and paid the price.
3. The smokescreen of saving the club from going out of business does not impress the fans. Mr McDougall, you blew it this season when the team had a good chance to establish itself in a higher league with a manager who is currently helping Clyde to replace Cowden in the First Division.
4. Be careful what you say about not taking supporters' money. Cowden had the lowest crowd in league football in Britain on Saturday. There is now hardly anyone from the local district

171

interested in the club.

5. Mr Harrow must be replaced by someone with more experience.

6. You say it takes time to build a successful team. It took 22 years after Cowden were relegated last time. Is there any point in keeping the football club going with Highland League clubs and even junior sides showing more ambition?"

As if to answer the charge of lack of ambition, Cowdenbeath announce the signing of a new player/assistant manager for a five figure fee. He is Colin 'Bomber' Harris, who has played with Raith Rovers, Hibs and latterly Hamilton Accies. Andy Harrow has been tracking him for some time, and sees him as the ideal man to bring out the best in his promising youngsters. The problem in securing Harris's signature has been that of finding employment for him in Fife. Gordon McDougall creates a job for him in his own business.

"Colin can play anywhere, although he made his name as a striker," says a delighted Andy Harrow, who played alongside Harris at Kirkcaldy. "He has played at a high level, and has had experience in a variety of roles. He will be a tremendous influence on the younger players.

"He will be a real leader on the park, and his vast experience will be of great value in coaching and training."

Cowdenbeath's sorry plight attracts the attention of the national media. Sky Television do a feature on the side with the worst record in Britain, and the newspapers are full of references to the joke team from Fife.

"It's amazing how much interest our plight has created among newspapers who normally only print our results," says the manager. "I hope they will show the same interest if we are doing well next season."

April 10. Cowdenbeath 0, Morton 1.

Another late goal! This time two minutes from the end – and it's the 100th Cowdenbeath have conceded this season. However, Cowden play well, and are unlucky to lose. Colin Harris's influence is immediately seen; the players respond to his prompting.

April 17. Cowdenbeath 0, Ayr United 1.

Another late goal. The attendance is an all-time low of 213 – lower even than the crowds Cowden were attracting during bad days in the Second Division. The manager is barracked as usual.

April 24. Raith Rovers 4, Cowdenbeath 1.

"Let's face it boys, we're shite" is the cry from a well-dressed man at the Cowdenbeath end of the stand. He obviously doesn't believe in the new psychology of affirmation.

When will the season end?

* * * * *

The season is at an end for the Scottish international team. They crash 5-0 in Portugal, saying farewell to the World Cup and inaugurating a new, yet familiar season of weeping and wailing and gnashing of teeth, a national version of "Let's face it boys, we're shite". The tormented breast-beating is itself a national sport, in which Scotland are regular championship winners. Newspapers and television are full of morbid analysis by experts. Jim Baxter is the name most frequently cited as a model of how it should be.

The womenfolk have seen it all before. But the new breed of Scottish feminists are not going to hold the menfolk's hands. No, not any more. Things have changed. This is a new Season, boys, and you'd better believe it.

"Scots football was a substitute for life, until last week," writes Dorothy-Grace Elder in a merciless column in *Scotland on Sunday*. Now it isn't good enough to be a substitute for death. Where can we find more suitable opponents for Scotland – perhaps one-legged Latvians, Greenland geriatrics or Monrovian mixed infants (all of whom will also gub them). Almost the entire United Nations have gubbed Scotland by now – is the invincibility of male madness still strong enough to ensure that the game which is so obviously a bogey continues in its present feverish form?

"Ashen-faced, sick as parrots and with their hair-dos seriously dented, the prancing princes of the field should not survive to fail another day. Yet the all-time showing up in Portugal may be the best thing that could happen to Scotland – I mean the country, not to be confused with 11 washouts in muddy knickers.

"Can't everyone see that this national opiate is a waste of time? Football is one of the most destructive monsters in Scots society. It starts with children dressed as beer cans absorbing hatred between the goalposts. It progresses to emasculating men, replacing proper patriotism with fleeting, fake fervour. The *toga virilis* has become the wet polyester strip, as grown men seek glory in the silliest places – on playing fields rather than in the league for big boys and girls....power and politics. Four hundred miles away, those who really run Scotland, the fans of the flannelled fools (another bunch of failures) are happy to see football sapping the virility of Scotsmen. It has nurtured a generation of political ballless wonders, obsessed with an airball instead of real life.

"Today's patriotic Scotsman would walk ten thousand miles to support the worst eleven, but is too lethargic to haul his shellsuit 300 yards to a polling booth. It is only during the summer break that he has time to notice his wife walked out last December.

"It is because I care for my country that I rejoice that this grotesque time–waster has now been gloriously gubbed in public esteem. Instead of throwing up, let's grow up. If football vanished completely (blessed thought) the only thing we'd miss would be the clichés....'Famous Scots victory' (goal-less draw); 'We are proud of our fans today – a real friendly match' (only 70 arrests); 'We're hoping for a result' (5-0).

"The most feeble excuse of all was that the grand old team was 'tired' in Portugal. What? Men who are very big men indeed, when they stand on their wallets, were tired? Oscar Wilde's 'game fit only for rough girls' could have done with some last week."

Ouch! Dorothy-Grace has kicked the corporate Scottish manhood where it hurts most. Her message is simple, and can be paraphrased as follows: Let's face it boys, *you're* shite.

* * * * * * *

A grey-haired, podgy Jim Baxter is all over the front pages of the *Sun,* under six-foot deep headlines, "I drank 21 bottles of Bacardi a Week".

The story begins: "Soccer legend Jim Baxter told yesterday how he nearly died after spending the last 30 years on the booze.

The ex-Rangers star downed 21 bottles of Bacardi a week at the peak of his addiction, before finally ending up in hospital. His body was bloated, his liver was about to give out. And stunned doctors told him that if he had kept on drinking he would have been dead within three days."

Jim, now 53, tells of how he thought he was about to die.

"I thought my time had come. But the truth is I didn't know a lot about it. I didn't see any pearly gates or anything like that. It's more likely that I was knocking on hell's gates."

When he was in hospital, old friends such as Billy McNeill, Ralph Brand and Jimmy Johnstone came to see him – "but a lot of the time I didn't know anyone was there. For more than a week I didn't know if it was New York or New Year. Ralphy told me later that he reckoned he was looking at a dead man.

"It used to be just one continuous drinking session. If I woke at four in the morning I would have a large vodka before going back to bed. The only decision I had to make when I left my house in the morning was which pub I was going to start the daily binge at. I didn't think of myself as an alcoholic – you don't when you're permanently under the influence.

"They say if you drink more than 21 units a week you are heading for trouble. Christ, I used to get through that by lunch

Not-so-slim Jim Baxter raises a glass of mineral water

time. Sometimes I had a bottle for breakfast and at my peak I was polishing off three bottles a day."

Not-so-slim Jim, who confesses that he has got through half a million pounds by way of drink and gambling, goes on: "I feel lucky that I've been given a second chance, and I aim to take it. I've got two choices – I can forget the bevy sessions, or I can kiss my ass goodbye. It's as simple as that.

"My lifestyle has cost me my health, and before that my marriage and my kids for a time. The fact is booze can cost you all the things that are nearest and dearest to you. But it's not too late for me and I don't plan to screw it up this time."

Jim, hang in there: there's still a lot to play for in your season.

* * * * *

It's end-of-season time for Britain's miners. *The Herald* sets it out:

"British Coal's controversial plan to axe 31 pits and 30,000 jobs is well on the way to fruition. By the end of this week, 17 collieries will have ceased production and more than 15,000 men will have quit the industry.

"Despite the defiant stand of the NUM leadership, demoralised miners are now queuing for 'voluntary' redundancy, encouraged by enhanced offers worth as much as £8000 over the national redundancy scheme. Such offers, made available for a brief period, were taken up by 2600 colliers last week, taking to 13,262 the total of mineworkers who have opted to go since the closure plans were announced last October. In addition, some 1300 white collar staff have also taken the money.

"Those tempted included the workforces at at least four of the ten most threatened pits. A further five pits ended production last week, and another two will shut on Friday."

Where are you, Winston Churchill?

So it's a final Goodnight to the British miners. And Good Morning to the child miners of Eastern Europe and Latin America.

We can all sleep easily in our beds now, knowing that our future fuel needs are in the safe, democratic hands of the nuclear overlords, the sheiks of the Middle East, the rising Fascists of Eastern Europe and South America.

Nice to know that the miners unions' long struggles against

slave conditions are over.

Nice to know that the power of the miners is finally broken, and we can all get our fuel that bit cheaper. Thirty pieces of silver per ton, perhaps?

Nice to know that Tarzan's political career has not been badly damaged, after all, by the unfortunate incidents of the last few months.

Nice to know that we live in progressive days.

Jesus wept.

The figures say it all: unemployment in Cowdenbeath is close on fifteen per cent. The number of unemployed claimants at the Cowdenbeath Job Centre is 2733. Fifty two people are chasing every vacancy.

"These figures spell misery and hardship for hundreds of families," says the local MP, Dr Gordon Brown. Councillor John Simpson comments: "There is no doubt we still have many unemployment blackspots throughout the district, with the Cow—denbeath area amongst the worst, with almost one in seven people out of work. It is quite clear that the Government's constantly changing economic policies are having no impact whatsoever."

Nearly 17,000 people in Fife are classed as unemployed, putting the kingdom well above the already high national figures. Fife has the fewest job opportunities per unemployed person of any Region in Scotland.

The *Fife Business Review* is bleak. Fife's employment base is contracting rapidly, it says. There has been a decline in inward investment by new businesses coming to Fife, it says. There is currently no hard evidence to indicate that an upturn in the Fife economy is imminent, it says. "It therefore seems very unlikely that, given the existing national framework, unemployment in Fife will be reduced to 'acceptable' levels in the near future."

The rise in Cowdenbeath's population from under 2000 to more than 11,000 this century was due to the coal rush. Since the collapse of the coal industry, there has been nothing to take its place. The Cowdenbeaths of the world have been tribal townships of black-dusted cheap, willing and ultimately expendable labour. They are the Sowetos of British industrial society, finally isolated on the top of coal bings nobody wants. Since the closure of the pits they have been looking down, in more ways than one, a black hole.

What is the biggest source of employment for working men and women in Cowdenbeath? The naval base and dockyard at Rosyth is the leading contender. It is estimated that some 18,000 jobs depend on the Rosyth complex which is worth £220 million to the local economy. Contraction at Rosyth would be devastating for Fife, which is the most defence-dependent region in Scotland.

Rumours of job losses at Rosyth sweep the county, despite all kinds of comforting Government noises. Mining communities have heard these sounds before. They do not trust them.

Which yard will win the Government contract for the refitting of the Trident nuclear submarine? Devonport or Rosyth? Apart from the merits or demerits of the respective bids, political correspondents point out that failure to award the contract to Devonport will put nine Conservative seats at risk, whereas Fife is safe Labour territory anyway...Is there a certain familiarity about these matters?

If the Rosyth workers are thrown to the wolves, the impact on West Fife will be devastating.

"It is clearly the case that the future of a large part of the local economy is tightly bound up with the effects of the decisions regarding the Rosyth complex," concludes the Fife Business Review. "It is difficult to over-emphasise the importance of the dockyard and the naval base to the Fife economy both across the economic sectors and throughout the region."

What about the promises? Ah, the promises.

Sir Nicholas Hunt, former Royal Navy Flag Officer, Scotland, remembers: "When I was here I gave the clearest of clear under-takings that, in return for the nuclear submarine base at Faslane, the work of maintenance and re-fitting would be done at Rosyth."

Lord Younger confirms. The promise of the Trident re-fitting work at Rosyth was the sugar coating on the bitter pill of Faslane. A devil's pact, but a public one, confirmed and confirmed over several years. Where have we heard this sort of talk before?

Come in, Bonar Law, your time's up in the letter and the spirit.

Sir Nicholas Fairbairn insists that the promises be kept. He prophesies that if they are not, every Tory seat in Scotland will be lost. He is wrong, of course. Life will go on, as usual. We are a nation of recidivists.

West Fife miners can well remember 'clearest of clear' undertakings. Lots of them. That's why everyone is counting their spoons. That's why there is fear in the community.

It is familiar, familiar, familiar. The smell of betrayal is everywhere. Been there. Now there again. To everything there is a season. Brothers and sisters, the Season of Betrayal is upon us again. Now Let Us Pray.

Will Ian Lang resign in protest at the almost inevitable body–swerve of these repeated promises? Surely such a decent, moral man will not permit his government to renege on clearly stated and reinforced pledges to the Scottish people. Will he not go?

Will Cowdenbeath win the European Cup?

The Secretary of State will make soothing noises, syrupy, balming, embalming, making betrayal sound like super news. That furrowed, concerned brow will go into action, sure sign that you are about to be sold – but sold with such urbane and concerned Hospital Trust bedside manner that you will think for a moment that you are being offered a marvellous cure rather than being given news with terminal implications. That earnest Scottish Colonial Brow will again go into overdrive as a further assault is made on local democracy in the plans for the re-organisation of local government.

The central state will increase its grip on the land through a further erosion of local accountability and the withholding of funds. Yet more government-appointed quangos, full of unelected ideological time-servers, will be appointed.

If the people revolt, why, the Riot Act can be read and the leaders thrown into prison. They will not, to be sure, rub shoulders with the likes of Ernest Saunders there: he was released from prison because of alleged premature senility and is now on the lecture circuit. The national silver has been sold off to hucksters in a land of sleaze and scams. Hello, Asil Nadir! Goodbye, Asil Nadir!

Apathy is now the problem: apathy born of repeated betrayal. People look on with glazed eyes as the assets of a nation's compassionate services are gradually stripped, and the poor are asked to pay the price of enormous fiscal mismanagement.

179

One thing is for sure: a struggling little football team cannot bear the sins and wounds and failures and burdens and desperations of a community which bears its name. Especially one with the smell of fear in its nostrils.

Unthinkable thought: what if the football team's defeat, its relegation, is symbol of a wider community defeat, a deeper wounding, a bigger slaughter, not just of its jobs, but of its hopes and dreams? One attack too many on its inner sense of meaning?

Let's face it, boys . . . .

. . . . isn't it time we tore up the national script?

Isn't it time we got up off our knees and stood as men and women of dignity and worth?

Listen. Switch off that chat show: it can wait. Put the new share offer in the drawer, meantime. And listen.

What is that sound you hear?

It is the sound of weeping.

* * * * *

Eric Archibald sits morosely at home in Cowdenbeath. He has just walked out on the club he loves passionately, and says he won't play for them again. He says that he has been sickened by the way things have been handled over the season, and what he sees as the unfair treatment of younger brother Alan, who was in the side for a few weeks, but no longer gets a game.

"I'm really sad that it's come to this," he says. "It's devastating to think that a year ago we were winning promotion. John Brownlie was right – we needed to buy three or four players to make a go of it. I don't think the board really wanted promotion in the first place. It's a sad day when the junior clubs are doing much better than Cowdenbeath."

Cowdenbeath Football Club announce that Tom Currie and John Marshall have resigned as directors. Both men deny that they have resigned. Further court action is threatened.

They say that Cowdenbeath Football Club have a new sponsor.

They say it's Oxo. To mark the occasion, Oxo have brought out a new product, they say.

It's called 'Laughing Stock'.

So you think that's funny?

May

The world is a gaming table so arranged that all who enter
the casino must play, and all must lose more or less heavily in
the long run, though they may win occasionally.
– Samuel Butler.

We will listen instead to the wind's text
Blown through the roof, or the thrush's song
In the thick bush that proved him wrong,
Wrong from the start, for nature's truth
Is primary, and her changing seasons
Correct out of a vaster reason
The vague errors of the flesh – R.S. Thomas.

MAY 1, 1993. Dunfermline Athletic 0, Cowdenbeath 2.

Gotcha! So who's the Laughing Stock noo?

To gub promotion-seeking neighbours Dunfermline, against all
the odds – and at East End Park too – is the kind of stuff which
drives the dark satanic fantasy mills of Cowdenbeath. Second top
of the league, and favourites to join fellow Fifers Raith Rovers in
the Premier league, Dunfermline have looked forward to entertaining Cowdenbeath in the bloodthirsty way that Dracula used to
anticipate playing host to succulent maidens. They expect to take
several goals off their poor neighbours, and their fans look forward to an afternoon of taunting the bloodied and not altogether
unbowed miniscule Cowdenbeath travelling support.

When the ground staff of East End park turn up for work on
Saturday morning, they find the words 'The Blue Brazil' daubed
on the pitch. Is this what makes the full-time Dunfermline players
start the game so nervously: a blue slogan like a curse on the
green sward? The writing is on the pitch for Dunfermline: they are
not going to win.

Twenty minutes into the second half, Eddie Petrie's long throw is knocked down by Iain Lee into the path of Willie Callaghan, who fires the ball high into the Dunfermline net. The centre-forward, who has had to endure the taunts of "Reject! Reject!" from the Dunfermline fans, does not conceal his delight at scoring against his former club. Dunfermline try to come back, but Bomber Harris prowls majestically at the back of the Cowdenbeath defence. There is no way through.

Cowdenbeath have several near misses: then, with two minutes to go, Callaghan races clear to score his second. The Cowdenbeath supporters dance with joy. Their team have, by beating their great rivals, doubled their league victories for the season: two wins in 42 games! The humiliated Dunfermline fans chorus abuse at their manager and demand that the board of directors resign. As they take a last look back at the pitch, the painted blue-on-green message torments them.

The *Central Fife Times* sums it up: "Forget about beating Partick Thistle and drawing with Hibs in the cup. This was the result the long-suffering Cowdenbeath fans have been waiting for. Beating the Auld Enemy with a bit of style went a long way to erasing the disappointments of this season, and for the loyal 100 or so Blue Brazil supporters who travelled to East End Park on Saturday it was a moment to savour."

Andy Harrow is euphoric.

"Everyone played well," he says, "and we showed that we can play a bit. To be honest, we were worth more than a two goal win, and I was delighted not only for the players but also our loyal band of fans who gave us great support. Colin Harris played in his defensive role quite brilliantly, but then everyone was brilliant on a great day for the club."

Everyone was brilliant! Can this be Cowdenbeath?

A rumour sweeps around the Cowdenbeath pubs that Brazil's past and present internationalists are so overawed by Cowdenbeath's scintillating destruction of Dunfermline's promotion hopes that Pele and company wish to be known henceforth as 'The Yellow Cowden'.

The rumour is as yet unconfirmed.

May 8: Cowdenbeath 0, Kilmarnock 3.

It takes Kilmarnock only four minutes to go ahead and stamp their authority on the game. Willie Lamont fumbles a Stark header, and the ball crosses the line, pleasing the large number of Killie fans in the 2750 crowd. Two goals follow fairly easily in the second half.

The defeat means that Cowdenbeath have not won at home the whole season - the first time this undesirable record has been achieved in thirty years.

May 15: St Mirren 1, Cowdenbeath 2.

Cowden finish a dreadful season on a high note! Callaghan and Henderson are the scorers. This is only Cowden's third win the whole season, all of them away from home, and two of them coming in the final three weeks of the season against promotion contenders.

Andy Harrow comments, "We got stuck in and although there were one or two close calls, I feel we were worth the win. It is a nice way to end the season, and gives us the confidence for next season."

The results mean that Dunfermline will not be promoted. They were favourites to go up until they were torpedoed by Cowdenbeath, who then ensured the Pars' fate by losing to Kilmarnock and beating contenders St Mirren. Cowdenbeath is not awash with tears.

It is announced that Jocky Scott, the Dunfermline manager, has been sacked. His replacement is Bert Paton, who was manager at Cowdenbeath for a few weeks.

Clyde win the Second Division championship, and look forward to life in the First Division. They are planning to strengthen their squad by signing some new players. Their assistant manager smiles. His name is John Brownlie.

Shoot Magazine, the big-circulation UK-wide football journal, has a two-page spread titled in huge letters "MAD COW DISEASE: COWDENBEATH - THEY'RE SO BAD IT'S UNBELIEVABLE".

"Poor Cowdenbeath managed to pick up almost every unwanted record going this season," it shrieks. It details the horrifying statistics of a nightmare season - first team in Britain to be relegated; team with the lowest number of points (13); team with lowest number of wins (3); only team never to win at home; team with the highest number of goals against (109).

The *Blue Brazilian* fanzine takes a look at the season. Its front page is taken up with a certificate, addressed to the manager of Cowdenbeath F.C.

"This award is normally given to individuals who have shown a great deal of courage and talent over a period of time. However, this year it is to be awarded to a man who came from nowhere and has achieved a First in his short career. It gives us much pleasure in presenting this year's award to Mr Andrew Harrow for being the first manager in British professional football to have his team relegated and getting a cracking bonus for fulfilling his contract with such efficiency and speed. Signed, U.R. Useless."

A league table illustrating the success records of Cowdenbeath managers over the years shows Andy Harrow rooted firmly at the bottom, with just over 13 per cent. John Brownlie is near the top, with a 57 per cent success record.

Included in '36 things never said at Central Park' are the following gems:

*"Cowdenbeath have turned down an offer for one of their top players"

*"The kick-off was delayed for five minutes to let the East Stirling travelling support into the ground"

*"Peter Lamont's tireless running and foraging was a feature of the game"

*"Keeper Lamont resisted the urge to bring down the onrushing striker"

*"Cowdenbeath rarely conceded goals in the last ten minutes"

*"Andy Harrow yet again picked up the Manager of the Month award"

Hugh Douglas and Willie Callaghan are chosen Players of the Year by the Kirkford Tavern branch of the Cowdenbeath Supporters' Club. Only one player is freed - Alan Archibald. Most of the promotion-winning side have already moved on. Seven players refuse terms - Eric Archibald, Colin Scott, John Wright, Nicky Henderson, Willie Herd, Billy Lamont and Sandy Robertson. The terms on offer are less money than the players were on during their last season in the Second Division. Cowdenbeath are a downwardly mobile club, living within their means but offering less than the Juniors.

* * * * * * *

Andy Harrow is like a man awakening from a nightmare. Is he still in one piece?

"I knew it would be hard," he tells me, "but I never knew it would be hard as this. The barracking got to me at times, but I had confidence in my own ability. Sometimes, I must admit, I felt like gesturing back. The fans can shout or bawl as much as they like, but if I were to respond, I'd get lifted."

What about the fans' view that the promotion-winning team had been destroyed and that their favourite, Peter Lamont, had not been given a fair chance?

"The players had never played in the First Division, and many of them simply weren't good enough, but I had to play them week after week. Peter Lamont was the most skilful player I had at Cowdenbeath, but his attitude to training wasn't good. If one player is allowed to get away with not training properly, it affects the rest of the team. The fact of the matter is that when Peter Lamont was on the transfer list, not a single club came for him."

How is he looking forward to next season?

"Very much. Our youth policy has been a real success. I've been able to sign good youngsters. I always say to promising young players that they'll get their chance at Central Park, and if they prove themselves they'll get a transfer to a bigger club. After all, I started with Cowdenbeath at 16, and I say to them –'See if you can beat me.'

"What I want at Central Park is a team of good young players, with a few experienced professionals who will teach them good habits. Colin Harris has made a great difference since he came here. He can play at the back or at the front, and he influences those round about him.

"Next season is a big test for me, because it will be my team.

There will be less pressure on us in the Second Division. I think we can do well."

Next season. It's like a drumbeat of hope against experience. I find myself looking forward to it already.

Is this a recognised, certifiable condition? Is it a deadly virus that attacks the brain?

The portakabins are gone at last, no tears. They have symbolised a depressing season. The diggers move in to lay the foundation of the new stand.

Like his manager, the chairman is optimistic about the future.

"I'm sure our youth policy is right," he says. "We'll have a reserve team again next season, and a youth side in the BP Cup. Paddy Dolan has been appointed youth coach, and he will work alongside Andy Harrow and Colin Harris. We'll continue to run Cowdenbeath Football Club within our means – that's the only way that the future of football can be secured.

"By the start of the season we hope to have a youth squad of sixteen players playing regularly to add to a first team squad of eighteen, and we want to be in a position to give the best of them an early chance of first team football. With this youth input added to the likes of Colin Harris, David Watt, Nicky Henderson and Willie Callaghan we have the basis of what will hopefully be a good squad of players which will do well in the Second Division next season, and there will be new senior recruits joining them."

Gordon McDougall tells me excitedly that the new cantilever stand – built with the insurance money and a grant from the Football Trust – will seat up to 600. This means that 1600 people will be under cover in the new and old stands. There will be new changing facilities, offices, hospitality lounge and boardroom, with facilities for functions.

The club has also made application to Dunfermline District Council for permission to develop the west end of the ground. The plans include an outdoor sports area, erection of fencing and floodlighting, and the construction of an access road. The idea is to transform the old 'cow shed' area into a seated enclosure. Seats from the old Murrayfield Rugby ground and the old Stirling

Albion stadium have been obtained, and are already at Central Park.

The chairman says that if the plans are approved and the funding package successfully completed, there will be an all-weather sports facility at the west end of the ground.

"We would have five five-aside football pitches there, which would be available for use by local people as well as schools," he says. "If we are successful with these plans, this, allied to the stand project and the improvements to the car park at the east end, will give Central Park a completely new look."

This is what the loyal supporters want to hear. It also gives the lie to the recurrent rumour that Gordon McDougall is not interested in football, and is simply running the ground down with a view to selling. As far as the fans are concerned, the chairman and the manager are still very much on probation after the débacle of the John Brownlie saga and the disastrous season – but things are heading in a more positive direction.

"We hope eventually to have seats for up to ten thousand people at Central Park," Gordon McDougall tells me. "I am starting at the west end of the ground, because that's where most of the stock car spectators gather. Some of the football fans may not like that, but the stock car racing is our bread and butter. It helps to keep the football club alive."

Lord Ewing suggests that the new stand be called 'The Alex Menzies Stand', after my boyhood hero. He tells me, "Ming was always willing to go the extra mile for Cowdenbeath. He never gave up from the beginning to the end of a game. He inspired everyone who had Cowdenbeath at heart both on the park and on the terracing.

"To call the new stand after Ming would be a good link from the past to the present and would be popular on the terracing. The board of directors badly need improved public relations, and this would be a good move in that direction."

One thing for sure: Ming would have wanted everyone to work together for the benefit of the club. Whatever the rights and wrongs of the catastrophic season, the only thing that makes sense for a small and vulnerable club in the midst of an economic and employment black hole is for everyone with the interests of the club at heart to pull together. The community has been going through a hard time ever since the pits closed: the football club, however fragile, is a symbol of defiant life. Yes, hope over experience. But when hope dies, the community dies with it.

The manager has made mistakes, but he deserves a proper chance. The new ground improvements will transform the old decaying arena. The chairman and board now have the chance to show that their policy of running a tight ship and bringing through local youngsters is the right one. They need the support of the whole community.

Above all, the young players themselves need to get the chance to prove themselves. The names to look out for next season are youngsters like Alan Combe, Dom Maratea, Barry McMahon, Eddie Petrie, Donald Stout and Kevin Bowmaker, who have all had outings in the First Division, and other lads such as Ally Hamilton, Roger Carr, Andrew Brash, Stephen Reid, and Paul Durkin. Is there a Craig Levein or a Jim Baxter there? If, in time, they can combine the lionheart of Big Ming with the skills of Hooky Leonard, the Blue Brazil will rise above the loss of the Black Diamonds and keep a flickering flame burning.

Harry Ewing has convinced me, easily. Let's have a new Ming dynasty to help restore the fortunes of Cowdenbeath.

A sportsman's dinner held in Lochgelly Town Hall to help pay for the Cowdenbeath youth team's visit to the summer youth tournament in Sweden raises nearly £3500. The speakers include Donald Findlay QC, the journalist Craigie Veitch, and Jack Dougary, son of the former Cowdenbeath manager. The evening is chaired by Jim Leishman.

Donald Findlay auctions three tickets for the Ibrox directors' box for Rangers' next European cup tie, and this raises £400. Says Cowdenbeath director Ian Fraser, "The support we received from our guests and the public was quite brilliant, and we cannot thank them enough."

The Scottish Football League announce that in season 1994/95, there will be four leagues of ten clubs each, instead of the present three divisions.

So next season, there is everything to play for. The bottom five clubs in the First Division will be relegated to the third league, with the Second Division champions being promoted. In the Second Division, the bottom eight clubs will drop a division. All this means that if Cowden were to win the Second Division championship next season, they would jump straight into the new First Division.

"This will make the Second Division extremely competitive next season with a big prize for the champions. Above all else the worst we want is to finish in the top six of the division. That is essential."

Being realistic: with a young and experimental side, winning a place in the top six, and avoiding a drop into the Scottish football basement, would be a considerable achievement.

* * * * * * *

The end of another season. I walk through the town.

The Co-operative is no more. It is now the home of the 'Cowdenbeath Business Centre', whatever in God's name that might be. Probably not one of the nerve-centres of the financial world, probably not in touch with Tokyo every day. No queues for 'divvies' now: when the Store goes, the old order has truly collapsed.

What about that other centre of Cowdenbeath power? The old Cowdenbeath Town House is now a housing branch office of Dunfermline District Council: the place where the red flag flew impudently and triumphantly is now a colonial outpost. A world ruled from Dunfermline! (But we destroyed them, 2-0).

The Cowdenbeath cinema, the sweaty old dream factory, is now the gleaming Mecca Bingo Hall. No more films. No more Cowdenbeath cowboys exiting bow-legged into the dark night, keeping eyes peeled for Lochgelly Indians. On past the new houses where the old Foulford Primary School – whatever happened to the deid burds?– used to resound to the shouts of children, and where the accordion-playing evangelist would hoarsely bellow a message of Good News mediated through the grotesque images of the slaughterhouse: up to the gap site where the sinking ship which went by the name of Beath High School

189

has finally dropped so far below the Stenhouse Street plumb line that it has had to be taken out of service.

Many of the council houses have fancy new doors and windows. Most have garages beside them. Some have 'For Sale' notices in the garden. Welcome to the property-owning democracy of Cowdenbeath.

Pity about the unemployed, though.

My boyhood feet take me towards the Kirk of Beath, where so much of the story of Cowdenbeath began. I sit in the silence, in the dark brown pews, communing with ghosts. Then out into the bright sunlight, into the graveyard, where Burke and Hare's men used to find the fleshly material for their masters' experiments. The gravestones tell the story of the community – of patriarchs and of pit tragedies and of radical politics and of football: and of the women who endured it all.

Founding fathers and mothers. Pollocks and Dougarys. And Fergusons. A crowded lair, generations jostling in the same six feet of clay....Alexander Ferguson, who died on April 23, 1960, aged 80 years...his son, Joseph Ferguson, who died on June 5, 1986, aged 82 years. Still, somewhere, showing how Hooky did it? And Alexina, wife of Joe, died July 17, 1971, aged 64 years. Now part of the communion of saints which honours the mothers as well as the fathers of the faith?

A touching note: 'In ever loving memory of Charles Carlow Reid (Charlie), March 6, 1941, aged five years'. Being a wealthy and prominent coal owner could not prevent the death of a beloved child, laid to rest only feet away from rebel miners locked out of the pits and banned from ever working in the Fife coalfields.

'In loving memory of Alexander Venters, who died April 30, 1959, aged 45 years, beloved husband of Helen Logan. Treasured memories.' If you listen intently, you can still hear the roaring of the crowd.

Then down to the old tree. The grave stone says, 'To the memory of Comrade Robert Allan, secretary of the ILP, erected by friends and associates within the working class movement.' In the same grave: David Scott, of 220 Perth Road,

Cowdenbeath, 'who died in the Lindsay Pit disaster, December 14, 1957, aged 53, beloved husband of Aminta Allan'. It was Aminta who took back the broken body of her hero. She died in 1976, aged 73. The picture comes back: the crowds of dark-suited miners, silent: the minister's voice, Greater love hath no man than this...and all because somebody lit a fag in a dank, underground cave full of black diamonds.

On to another part of Beath cemetery. A small headstone is what I am looking for. I scrape it to let the lettering speak.

'In loving memory of our dear son and brother, Andrew Cree, killed June 9, 1947.'

Well, did He come to take up his jewels, precious jew-ells, bright gems for His crown? Does Andrew, slain by the Kirkford bus, his innards strewn along Cowdenbeath High Street some forty six years ago, shine like a star of the morning?

Well? If there's anything I can't stand, sonny boy, it's those preachers who won't Stand Up and Be Counted....

I answer in the affirmative in my heart. There.

Then there's a coughing in my lungs. Coal dust. German bombers. The Kirkford bus. An arm hanging out of a car on an unspeakably silent Kelty road. The motionless wheels as the bodies are laid out at the pithead: the dried-up tears on the black-dusted cheeks.

In the beginning was the Dream. And the dream was of a new Season: in another kingdom: beyond the kingdom of Fife.

Over the wall from the cemetery, the boys, and some 'rough girls' of the new – and level – Beath High School shout and run.

And play football.

The legendary 'Hooky' Leonard